The selected poems of DU FU

TRANSLATIONS FROM THE ASIAN CLASSICS

the selected

burton watson

poems of DU FU

COLUMBIA UNIVERSITY PRESS NEW YORK

COLUMBIA UNIVERSITY PRESS

Publishers Since 1893

New York Chichester, West Sussex

Library of Congress Cataloging-in-Publication Data

Du, Fu, 712–770.

The selected poems of Du Fu / Burton Watson.

p. cm.—(Translations from the Asian classics)

Includes bibliographical references.

ISBN 0–231–12828–2 (alk. paper)—

ISBN 0–231–12829–0 (pbk. : alk. paper)

1. Du, Fu, 712–770—Translations into English.

I. Watson, Burton, 1925– II. Title. III. Series.

PL2675.A276 2002

895.1'13—dc21

2002073778

Columbia University Press books are
printed on permanent and durable
acid-free paper.

Printed in the United States of America

Designed by Linda Secondari

c 10 9 8 7 6 5 4 3 2 1

p 10 9 9 7 6 5 4 3 2 1

contents

chronology

712	Born in Gong District, Henan. Father, Du Xian, a minor official.
731–735	Period of youthful wandering in area of Jiangsu and Zhejiang (Wu and Yue).
735	Goes to Chang'an to take *jinshi* examination; fails exam.
736–740	Period of wandering in Shandong and Hebei (Qi and Zhao).
741	Returns to Luoyang area.
744–745	Friendship with Li Bai in Luoyang area.
746	Goes to Chang'an.
747	Takes special exam given by Emperor Xuanzong. Due to machinations of chief minister Li Linfu, all candidates fail.
750	In Chang'an. Eldest son Zongwen born.

753	Second son Zongwu (Pony Boy) born.
755	Outbreak of An Lushan Rebellion. Luoyang falls to rebels.
756	Flees the rebels with his family; settles wife and family at Qiang Village in Fuzhou, north of capital. Emperor Xuanzong flees Chang'an, relinquishes throne to son, Emperor Suzong. Du Fu attempts to reach court of Suzong but is captured by rebels, detained in Chang'an.
757	In fourth month, escapes Chang'an, reaches court of Suzong at Fengxiang, is appointed Reminder. Incurs imperial displeasure for defending Fang Guan. Ordered to join family in Fuzhou. In eleventh month returns to Chang'an, now in government control.
758	In Chang'an in post of Reminder. In sixth month banished to minor post in Huazhou east of capital.
759	Leaves Huazhou in seventh month because of famine, travels west to Qinzhou. In tenth month goes to Tonggu. At end of year travels west to Chengdu in Sichuan.
760	Moves into thatched hall at Wash-Flower Stream in Chengdu.
762	To escape rebellion in Chengdu, moves to Zizhou.
764	Returns to Chengdu, takes post in local government.
765	Resigns post, returns to thatched hall. In fifth month leaves Chengdu with family, journeys down Yangzi River to Yun'an.

766 Travels down Yangzi to Kuizhou, moves into "western lodge."

767 Moves to Rangxi, later to East Camp in Kuizhou.

768 Leaves Kuizhou, goes down Yangzi to Yueyang in Hunan.

769 Travels in Lake Dongting area.

770 In Tanzhou in Hunan. Hopes to travel on to Chang'an but dies in Tanzhou region near end of year.

Introduction

Du Fu, the eliciter of superlatives! The Chinese scholar William Hung, who wrote the definitive book in English on Du Fu's life and poetry, gave it the unequivocal title *Tu Fu: China's Greatest Poet*. Professor Stephen Owen of Harvard, the leading American authority on Chinese poetry of the Tang period, enthusiastically seconds Hung's estimation of Du Fu. And the American poet and translator Kenneth Rexroth, who rendered some of Du Fu's poems in English, goes a step further to declare him "the greatest non-epic, non-dramatic poet who has survived in any language."[1]

My aim in the present volume is neither to question nor to confirm these judgments, but simply to present a selection of Du Fu's works in translation, though later in this introduction I would like to examine some of the reasons that could be cited to support these claims to greatness. Some fourteen hundred poems attributed to Du Fu have come down to us, but his fame rests mainly on one hundred or so poems that have been widely admired, commented on, and anthologized over the centuries by the Chinese and other peoples within the Chinese cultural sphere. My own selection of 135 poems includes translations of most of the poems for which he is best remembered along with a few less famous works that I believe deserve notice.

Du Fu's poetry was profoundly influenced by the troubled times in which he lived; before considering the poems themselves, it may therefore be helpful to give a brief summary of his life. Little biographical information regarding him has survived, and almost all of what we know of him comes from his own poems and other writings. A chronological outline of his life will be found on pp. vii–viii, but even some of the data listed there is conjectural in nature, as is much of the dating of the poems in my selection.

Du Fu came from a distinguished family of literati. His most illustrious ancestor was Du Yu (222–284), a literary leader and Confucian scholar who compiled an authoritative commentary on the *Zuozhuan*, one of the most important historical texts of the Confucian canon. Also of prominence was his paternal grandfather, Du Shenyan (d. 708), an official in the Tang bureaucracy and one of the outstanding poets of his time. Du Fu's father, Du Xian, also held an official post, though a minor one, and little is known of him. Du Fu's mother, whose surname was Cui, apparently died shortly after he was born; the younger brothers and sister he mentions in his poetry are almost certainly children by a second wife.

Du Fu, whose courtesy name was Zimei, was born in 712, one year before Emperor Xuanzong came to the throne. His place of birth is uncertain, but it is usually listed as Gong District in the Luoyang area of Henan. Almost nothing is known of his early years, though being the son of a family that for successive generations had held official posts, he no doubt worked diligently to prepare for the civil service examinations that opened the way to such offices. This involved intensive study and memorization of the classics of Confucianism, the standard histories, and literary works such as the voluminous *Wenxuan*, or *Literary Anthology*. He was well versed in Daoist literature as well and, as he himself mentions, at some point studied the doctrines of the Chan, or Zen, school of Buddhism and acquired a considerable knowledge of Buddhist writings.[2]

In his poems he refers to two periods of youthful wandering, the first, probably in the years around 731–735, to Jiangsu and the seacoast area of Zhejiang, and the second some years later to the northeast region of Shandong and Hebei. At some point, probably in 735, he went to the capital, Chang'an, to take the examination for *jinshi*, or Presented Scholar. Much to the bafflement of scholars and admirers of later generations, he failed to make a passing grade.

During his youthful years in the Luoyang area, when he was already very active as a poet, he became acquainted with a number of well-known literary figures, among them the famous poet Li Bo or Li Bai (701–762), whom he greatly admired. In several poems in my selection, Du Fu recalls their period of friendship and expresses concern over the older poet's welfare.

In 746 Du Fu left the Luoyang area and moved to Chang'an, living in a suburb of the city called Duling, where a number of families with the Du surname were located. Apparently he hoped to advance his chances for an official appointment by showing his writings to influential people in the capital and appealing to them for help, a common practice at the time among young men with literary and political ambitions. In a poem presented to one such patron, he describes himself wryly as "mornings rapping at some rich fellow's gate, / evenings trailing in the dust of his fat horses." (See poem 5.)

The period of Du Fu's youth, which corresponds to the early years of Emperor Xuanzong's reign, was one of widespread peace and prosperity, a golden age in the annals of Chinese culture. But by the time he moved to Chang'an, there were clear signs of impending disaster. The Chinese armies garrisoning the borders were, in many areas, pushing to extend the territory under Tang control and meeting with strong resistance from non-Chinese peoples such as the Turks, Tibetans, and Uighurs. The government resorted to harsh impressment measures to keep the armies fully manned, taking peasants from their homes and families for long periods of military duty.

Emperor Xuanzong, earlier so zealous in his attention to state affairs, had become concerned largely with two things: a Daoist-inspired pursuit of immortal life and his infatuation with a concubine named Yang Guifei. He showered wealth and honor on her and her relatives, the Yang family. Increasingly, he left political matters to his chief minister Li Linfu and, after Li's death in 753, to his successor Yang Guozhong, a cousin of Yang Guifei. Many of Du Fu's best-known works from this period deal with these problems—depictions, often in ballad form, of the sufferings caused by the impressment of men into military service or satires on the favors enjoyed by members of the Yang family.

In 747, shortly after his move to Chang'an, Du Fu had a second opportunity to try his luck at the civil service examinations when Emperor Xuanzong held a special exam for the purpose of discovering unrecognized talent. However, the chief minister Li Linfu, sensing a possible threat to his power, saw to it that all the candidates were given failing grades. It was not until late in 755 that Du Fu was at last assigned to a post in the government, a minor one in the palace of the Heir Apparent. The time was not auspicious for anyone joining the ranks of the Tang bureaucracy.

Toward the close of 755, An Lushan, a trusted military leader whose base of power was in the northeast in the area of present-day Beijing, initiated a revolt, ostensibly for the purpose of punishing the evil chief minister Yang Guozhong. His forces, sweeping west, captured Luoyang, the Eastern Capital, and before long they were pressing toward Chang'an. In the sixth month of 756, Emperor Xuanzong and his court fled the city by a western gate. When they reached Mawei, a little west of the capital, the soldiers escorting them killed Yang Guozhong and refused to go farther until the emperor agreed to have Yang Guifei put to death as well. The emperor reluctantly gave his consent, and she was taken to a nearby Buddhist chapel and strangled. Before retreating to safety in Sichuan, the emperor relinquished the throne to the Heir Apparent, who became Emperor Suzong and set up a temporary government in a remote area northwest of Chang'an.

Du Fu, by now married and the father of a family, fled the capital around the same time, journeying north, as he describes in the poem "Ballad of Pengya," and eventually he settled his wife and children at a place called Qiang Village in Fuzhou. He then attempted to make his way to the new emperor's headquarters, but was captured by the rebels and returned to Chang'an, where he was held under surveillance. In the fourth month of 757, he managed to escape from Chang'an and reach Fengxiang, west of the capital, where Emperor Suzong had established his court. As a reward for his loyalty, he was assigned the office of Reminder, an advisory post. In this post he quickly incurred the ruler's displeasure by speaking out in defense of Fang Guan, a high official and old friend who had fallen out of favor. He was relieved of his duties and ordered to join his family in Fuzhou. He later returned to Chang'an, once more in government hands, and was restored to the post of Reminder.

Du Fu apparently continued to do too much "reminding" for the emperor's taste, and, in the sixth month of 758, he was transferred to a lesser post in Huazhou east of the capital. Late in the year he made what was to be his last trip back to the Luoyang area that he called home.

By this time, An Lushan, the instigator of the rebellion, had been murdered by his son, but the rebel forces continued to pose a threat and contributed to the highly unstable condition of the empire. In the seventh month of 759, because of famine in the immediate area, Du Fu resigned his post in Huazhou and traveled west with his family in search of food, stopping for a time in Qinzhou, an outpost on the western frontier of the empire in present-day Gansu, then moving to Tonggu, and finally to Chengdu, a large city in the region of Shu, or Sichuan.

During much of his life, Du Fu seems to have been torn between two conflicting ideals: a high-minded and admirably Confucian desire to serve his sovereign and country as a member of the bureaucracy and a more Daoist-oriented wish to retire to the countryside to a life of rustic seclusion. He alludes frequently to both ideals in his poetry. During his stay in the Chengdu area, he was, to some extent, able to realize the second of these ideals, and the years he spent there were, relatively speaking, among the most peaceful and happy of his adult life.

Through friends, some highly placed in the local government, he and his family were able in 760 to settle in a small "thatched hall" on Wash-Flower Stream west of Chengdu, a site that has now become a veritable national shrine to the poet's memory. Because of a local rebellion, he was obliged to leave his house in 762 and take refuge in nearby Zizhou, but he returned to Chengdu in 764. For a brief time thereafter, he held a post in the local government but soon retired because of poor health.

The following year, 765, he left Chengdu and began traveling east down the Yangzi River, stopping at various points along the way. The many poems preserved from this period of his life allow a more accurate reconstruction of his movements, as is evident from the headings of poems in my selection. By 769 he had journeyed down the Yangzi as far as Lake Dongting in Hunan.

His health, never robust, was failing badly—he suffered from a lung ailment, probably asthma, was deaf in one ear, unsteady on his feet, and troubled by weakening eyesight. Plagued by constant worries over how to provide for his family, his declining health, and the uncertain fate of the nation, he often sinks into a mood of unrelieved melancholy in the poetry of these last years, constantly returning to themes of remoteness, of being far from "home." Late 770 found him in Tanzhou, the modern city of Changsha, southeast of Lake Dongting, still hoping to journey on to his homeland in the east, when death brought an end to his trials.

William Hung, in the work mentioned earlier, writes of Du Fu that he "appeared to be a filial son, an affectionate father, a generous brother, a faithful husband, a loyal friend, a dutiful official, and a patriotic subject."[3] Given all these sterling qualities, and the close links that traditional Chinese thought posits between art and morality, the implication is that he could hardly be anything but a great poet as well. The picture we have of him derives almost entirely from his own poems. Yet so convincing is that picture in its air of profound moral sincerity that, at least from Song times on, admiration for the poet's character has constantly complemented, and at times has even outshone, the literary evaluation of his writings. It is this admiration that is largely responsible for a twelfth-century critic's crowning him with the title *shisheng*, or "Sage of Poetry," making him the artistic counterpart of Confucius himself.

A second epithet frequently bestowed on him, that of "poet-historian," is similarly based less on literary considerations than on the large amount of historical information contained in his works. From the poems we acquire invaluable insights into the unsettled times in which he lived and vivid, detailed data regarding the lives of the common people, information of a kind seldom found in the officially compiled histories of the era.

Regarding the purely literary qualities that have won Du Fu's work its place of unrivaled eminence, we may note first the great variety of poetic forms in which he excelled. As one recent critic states, Du Fu "employed every prosodic form available to the Tang poet and, depending upon the state in which he found a particular prosodic form, either made outstanding advances or contributed outstanding examples."[4]

My selection is limited to translations of his works in *shi* form, both the "old style" *shi* forms and the "new style," or tonally regulated forms. The latter include the four-line *jueju*, the eight-line *lüshi*, or regulated verse, and the *pailü*, which is unrestricted in length. (The form and line length of the original are noted in the headings to my translations.) Du Fu also wrote works in the *fu*, or rhyme-prose form, though his efforts in this form are seldom read today.

In addition to its prosodic breadth and variety, Du Fu's work is distinguished by a similarly impressive breadth of subject matter. Something of this vast thematic variety is reflected in my selection, and further selections could be added to provide even more striking evidence of the multitude of themes he treated.

A corresponding richness is observable in Du Fu's language, which ranges from the elegant, highly polished diction of earlier court poetry to colloquialisms of the poet's own day, from language that is studied and heavily allusive to that which is startlingly direct and "unpoetic." He demonstrated that virtually all levels of language could be accommodated in the poem.

The thematic and stylistic comprehensiveness of Du Fu's work was one of the first qualities to be noted by critics. In 813, Du Fu's grandson, Du Siye, requested that Yuan Zhen, a distinguished poet and official, write an epitaph for his grandfather's grave. In Yuan's brief account of Du Fu, the earliest outside source we have on the poet, he singled out this quality in Du Fu's work for particular praise, noting that "he commanded all the traits displayed by poets of old, and could do all the things that present day poets do only singly."

Another salient feature of Du Fu's work is the inventiveness with which he wielded this masterful command of varied themes and styles. Thus, in a certain poetic form he treated subjects that had previously been thought suitable only for other forms, or he combined within a single form a variety of subjects that would earlier have been regarded as incompatible. His style and diction likewise show a chameleon-like tendency, contributing to what Stephen Owen has characterized as Du Fu's "shifting style."[5] So great was Du Fu's command of the language and literary tradition that he could elect to write on any theme or in any manner he chose, combining themes or styles in ways that were wholly without precedent. Even in the difficult closing years of his life, his work is tirelessly innovative and experimental. His expressed aim was to do what had never been done. As he states in a poem written in Chengdu in 761 (not included in my selection), "Perverse by nature, I'm addicted to fine lines; / if my words don't startle people, I won't give up till I die."[6]

One other characteristic of Du Fu's poetry merits particular notice, since it helps to explain the perennial appeal of his work—his realism. I will illustrate this by quoting a famous passage from a long poem entitled "Northern Journey," not included in my selection. The poem was written in the fall of 757, when Du Fu, having incurred Emperor Suzong's displeasure, was ordered to leave the court and travel north to Fuzhou, where his wife and children were living. The poem, 140 lines long, shifts back and forth between the political concerns of the entire nation and Du Fu's private family affairs. The following section, lines 59 to 88, shows us the scene that confronted the poet when, after a long and difficult journey, he finally reached the country house where his family was lodging:

> A year gone by, arriving at my thatched hut,
> wife and children, clothes a hundred patches:
> our cries mingle with the voice of the pines;
> the sad fountain joins our muffled sobbings.
> The little boy we've spoiled all his life,
> face paler, whiter than snow,
> sees his Papa, turns away in tears,
> dirty, grimy, feet with no socks.
> By the bed my two young girls,
> mended skirts scarcely covering their knees,
> a sea scene, the waves chopped up,
> bits of old embroidery sewn all askew,
> marine monster, purple phoenix

topsy-turvy on their coarse cloth jackets.
Old husband, feeling somewhat poorly,
vomiting, runny bowels, several days laid up in bed.
But don't think I've no fabrics in my bag
to save you from the shakes and shivers of the cold!
Here's powder and mascara—I'll unwrap them—
quilts, coverlets—I'll lay them all out.
The face of my thin wife regains its brightness;
my silly girls start in combing their own hair.
They copy all the things they've seen their mother do,
step by step applying morning makeup,
taking their time, smearing on rouge and powder—
how ridiculous—drawing eyebrows this wide!
But I'm home alive, facing my young ones,
and it's as though I've forgotten about hunger and thirst.
They keep asking questions, outdoing each other in pulling
  my beard,
but who'd have the heart to scold them?

It would appear that at this time Du Fu had four children, two girls and two boys. The "little boy" in line 5 of my excerpt is probably his younger son, Pony Boy. It seems odd that he should turn away from his father in tears, though perhaps through some misunderstanding he thinks he has done something for which he will be scolded. The "old husband" in line 15 is, of course, Du Fu himself.

The whole passage, replete with closely observed details, has two sections of particular note. The first is Du Fu's description of the clothes worn by the girls, garments that Du Fu's wife has mended with patches cut from an old and probably expensive piece of embroidery. The embroidery originally depicted a seascape complete with the mythical sea monster called Tian Hu and a purple phoenix or purple phoenixes. But the pattern has now been cut to bits and sewn so that the figures are askew or upside down. The crazy quilt effect that results perfectly reflects the disruption and chaos that have descended on the Du family, and by extension on the whole of Tang China. The second notable section occurs in the latter part, when the little girls, seizing on the powder and mascara that the poet has brought for his wife, proceed to plaster their faces with it. The mood here is all gaiety and madcap humor, a brief moment of brightness before the poem quits the domestic scene and turns to solemn concerns of national policy.

Earlier poets allowed brief glimpses of their family life or their everyday activities in their poems, but they wrote nothing to compare to the concreteness and intimacy of such passages as this by Du Fu. They are among the most memorable and widely quoted in all his works and exercised an inestimable influence on the Chinese poetic tradition of later times.

A perceptive person reading Du Fu in the original would presumably be able to respond to the excellent qualities outlined above and appreciate the true literary worth of his work. But what of a person reading Du Fu in translation? Regrettably, Du Fu has long been known as the despair of translators; as David Hawkes observes dryly, "his poems do not as a rule come through very well in translation."[7] Part of the difficulty stems from the "shifting style" mentioned earlier. A poem may capture one mood for a time and then quite abruptly veer into another, may open with a vision of all-encompassing grandeur but close on a relatively narrow and solipsistic note. Du Fu's acute sensitivity seems to keep his attention darting from one aspect of a scene to another, and his emotional response shifts accordingly.

He was especially skillful in his use of the eight-line *lüshi*, or regulated verse form, and many examples will be found in my selection. The form demands strict verbal parallelism in the second and third couplets, and the deft and highly original manner in which Du Fu shapes these parallelisms is one of the wonders of his art. But such parallelisms—and they are used extensively in his poems in other prosodic forms as well—often tend to sound forced or mechanical in translation, particularly as modern poetry so seldom employs rhetorical devices of this sort. Moreover, poems in regulated verse form are frequently so compressed in language and so devoid of syntax that in translation they seem almost clogged with images, static and unflowing. Some translators attempt to lessen the studied effect of parallelisms by deliberately blurring their symmetry, or they try to relieve the monotony of end-stopped lines by converting some into run-on lines. Though I can understand the impulse behind such procedures, in my own translations I have endeavored in most cases to stick as closely as possible to the wording and lineation of the original.

There are many different ways to approach the problems involved in translating Du Fu, which is why we need as many different translations as possible. Any attempt to achieve a translation of his poetry that is wholly satisfactory is an exercise in the impossible, yet even a translation that is only partially successful seems eminently worth striving for. Such is the power and appeal of Du Fu's work and the importance of its place in world literature that translators, myself among them, will always keep trying.

Some of these translations appeared earlier in my *Columbia Book of Chinese Poetry* (1984) and *Renditions: A Chinese-English Translation Magazine*, no. 55 (spring 2001) and are reproduced here in slightly revised form.

NOTES

1. William Hung, *Tu Fu: China's Greatest Poet* (Cambridge, Mass.: Harvard University Press, 1952). Stephen Owen, *The Great Age of Chinese Poetry: The High T'ang* (New Haven: Yale University Press, 1981), p. 183. Kenneth Rexroth, *One Hundred Poems from*

the Chinese (New York: New Directions, 1956), p. 135. In my earlier works on Chinese literature I have used the Wade-Giles system of romanization, which renders the great poet's name as Tu Fu. In this volume I switch to the pinyin system now used in China, which renders his name as Du Fu.

2. In an early poem entitled "Night: Hearing Xu Eleven Recite Poems; in Admiration I Wrote This," Du Fu says, "I too made Can and Ke my teachers." Can and Ke are Huike and Sengcan, second and third patriarchs of the Chinese Chan or Zen school of Buddhism. These men lived in the sixth century, so Du Fu must mean either that he studied the writings attributed to them or that he studied with men who were successors to their teaching line.

3. William Hung, *Tu Fu*, p. 282.

4. Eva Shan Chou, *Reconsidering Tu Fu: Literary Greatness and Cultural Context* (Cambridge: Cambridge University Press, 1995), p. 56.

5. Stephen Owen, *Chinese Poetry*, p. 192.

6. In a poem entitled "Along the River, Finding Its Waters as Powerful as an Ocean, Which Led to These Brief Remarks."

7. David Hawkes, *A Little Primer of Tu Fu* (Oxford: Oxford University Press, 1967), p. ix.

The selected poems of Du Fu

Evening Banquet at Mr. Zuo's Villa

(5-character regulated verse. The date and location of the poem are uncertain, as is the identity of Mr. Zuo.)

1

Wind-tossed trees, a slim moon setting,
robes dew-damp, the clear tuning of a *qin*:[1]
hidden waters flow by blossomed pathways,
spring stars encircle the thatched hall.
We examine books till the candles burn low,
admire swords, leisurely sipping wine,
then, poems done, listen to songs of Wu—
never will I forget my lone boat travels there![2]

---

1. The *qin* is a horizontal stringed instrument like a zither or Japanese *koto*.
2. Du Fu is recalling his youthful wanderings in the region of Wu on the southeast coast. Throughout his poetry, the boat is a powerful symbol of freedom and escape.

Officer Fang's Barbarian Steed

(5-ch. regulated verse, around 741. Ferghana in Central Asia was renowned for its fine horses.)

2

Barbarian steed, pride of Ferghana,
all jags and angles, well-knit bones;
two ears cocked, like bamboo tubes split sideways;
four hoofs fleet, as though buoyed on the wind.
Wherever headed, no distance too challenging,
fit indeed for a life-or-death charge.
With a mount superlative as this,
ten-thousand-mile sorties are at your command!

The Painted Hawk

(5-ch. regulated verse, probably around 742.)

3

Wind and frost swirl up from the white silk surface,
so superb, this painting of the gray hawk!
Shoulders hunched, he schemes to outwit the
  wily rabbit;
peers to one side like a vexed barbarian.
Foot cord and ring, a gleam bright enough to grasp;
by pillar and eaves, poised to come if you should call.
When will he swoop down on those lesser birds,
feathers and blood splattered over the barren plain?

On a Spring Day Thinking of Li Bai

(5-ch. regulated verse; written around 746, when Du Fu was in Chang'an near the Wei River and Li Bai was in the region of Wu southeast of the Yangzi.)

4

Li Bai—poems unrivaled,
thought soaring airborne, never banal:
the freshness, newness of Yu the Commander,
the rare excellence of Adjutant Bao.[1]
Here by the northern Wei, springtime trees;
east of the Yangzi, clouds at the close of day—
when will we share a cask of wine,
once more debate the subtleties of the written word?

---

1. Yu Xin (513–581), who held the title of Commander Unequaled in Honor, and Bao Zhao (414–466), who held a military post late in life, were two of the most distinguished poets of the period preceding the Tang.

Twenty-two Rhymes Presented to Assistant Secretary of the Left Wei

(5-ch. old style, written probably in 748 or 749, when Du Fu was in Chang'an, and presented to Wei Ji, an eminent official and litterateur who held the post of Assistant Secretary of the Left in the Department of State Affairs. Du Fu's family had been acquainted with the Wei family for several generations, and Du Fu himself, as the poem indicates, enjoyed the favor and patronage of Wei Ji. While thanking Wei Ji for his support and lamenting his own unworthiness, Du Fu is clearly hinting at his desire for continued patronage, though the close of the poem pictures him as ready to quit the capital in despair. The poem offers an invaluable insight into Du Fu's personality and ambitions—his immense self-confidence, here humorously expressed but at times bordering on arrogance; his longing for official position and the lofty goals he hoped to achieve thereby; and the intense frustration he felt over his inability to pass the exam and get ahead in the world.)

5

Those in silk underpants rarely die of hunger,
but a scholar's cap can bring its wearer much mishap.
Kind sir, please listen attentively
while a humble man states his case.
In the past, when I was still young,
already chosen a candidate for the exam,
reading books, I polished off ten thousand volumes,
wielded my writing brush like a god,
in rhyme-prose hailed the rival of Yang Xiong,
in poetry rated akin to Cao Zhi;
Li Yong desired to make my acquaintance,
Wang Han begged to move in next door.[1]
I too thought myself quite exceptional,

fit at once to climb to high office,
to lift my ruler higher than Yao and Shun,
restore the purity of the people's ways.
Those hopes ended in bleak despair,
though I go on singing, no hider from the world.[2]
Thirty years astride a donkey,
I take what there is to eat in the springtime capital,
mornings rapping at some rich fellow's gate,
evenings trailing the dust of his fat horses.
Leftover wine, a bit of cold roast,
and everywhere this sorrow I bear in silence.
Not long ago the sovereign held a levy;
suddenly here was my chance for advancement![3]
But in the blue sky my wings failed me;
I couldn't swim as fast as others in the shoal,
so ashamed to betray your generosity,
so certain, however, that you truly understand.
Always among the host of officials
you deign to recite the newest of my fine lines.
Like Gong Yu, I dare to delight in a friend's success,
but find it hard to endure Yuan Xian's poverty.[4]
How, with a mind so darkly downcast,
can I go on merely hopping this way and that?
My wish now is to retire to eastern seas,
leave this western land of Qin,
though still I long for the Zhongnan hills,
turn my head toward the banks of the clear Wei.[5]
Always I try to repay even small favors;
how not regret parting from my high official friend?
White gull in the vastness of the waves—
ten thousand miles away, who can tame him?[6]

1. Yang Xiong (53 B.C.E.–18 C.E.) was famous for his works in the *fu* or rhyme-prose form, Cao Zhi (192–232) for his poems in the *shi* form. Li Yong and Wang Han were eminent literary figures in Du Fu's father's generation.
2. Meaning uncertain; perhaps he is saying that, though he writes songs, he is not a recluse like the madman Jie Yu of Confucius' time, who sang prophetic songs.
3. In 747 Emperor Xuanzong held a special exam for candidates for official position, but Du Fu and all the others who took it were flunked through the machinations of the chief minister, Li Linfu.
4. When Gong Yu's friend Wang Yang was appointed to office, Gong Yu dusted off his hat, hopeful that he too would be appointed. Yuan Xian, a disciple of Confucius, was famous for the impoverished condition in which he lived.
5. The Zhongnan hills south of Chang'an and the Wei River north of the capital are both regions noted for their natural beauty.
6. Some texts read "White gull lost in the vastness" for the next to the last line. Either way, in this final couplet Du Fu imagines himself in the "eastern seas," free at last from all care.

Ballad of the War Wagons

(7-ch. and 5-ch., old style. Though the poem imitates the style of older works in *yuefu*, or ballad form, the title and content of the poem are original to Du Fu. Probably written around 750, the poem voices harsh criticism of the frequent recruiting of peasants to fight in Emperor Xuanzong's border wars.)

6

Rumble-rumble of wagons,
horses whinnying,
war-bound, bow and arrows at each man's waist,
fathers, mothers, wives, children running alongside,
dust so thick you can't see Xianyang Bridge,[1]
snatching at clothes, stumbling, blocking the
road, wailing,
wailing voices that rise straight up to the clouds.
From the roadside, a passer-by, I question the recruits;
all they say is, "Again and again men drafted!
Some sent north at fifteen to guard the Yellow River,
at forty still manning garrison farms out west.
When they set out, the village headman tied their
turbans for them;
they come home white-haired and draw border duty
again!
Border posts washed in blood, enough to make a sea,
but the Martial Sovereign's not yet done 'expanding
his borders.'[2]
You've never seen them?
Our Han land's two hundred districts east of the
mountains,
a thousand villages, ten thousand hamlets gone to
thorns and brambles!

Sturdy wives can handle plow and mattock,
but the rows of grain never come up quite right.
What's worse, we men of Qin, renowned as
tough fighters,
they herd us into the ranks like dogs and chickens![3]
You, sir, ask these questions,
but recruits like us hardly dare grumble out loud.
Still, in winter this year,
troops from here, West of the Pass, not yet disbanded,
officials started pressing for taxes—
tax payments—where would they come from?
Now you know why it's no good to have sons,
much better have daughters instead!
Sire a daughter, you can marry her to a neighbor;
sire a son and he ends buried under a hundred grasses.
You've never seen what it's like in Koko Nor?[4]
Years now, white bones no one gathers up,
new ghosts cursing fate, old ghosts wailing,
skies dark, drizzly rain, the whimpering,
whimpering voices."

---

1. The bridge over the Wei River north of Chang'an; the men are being sent west, probably to the Tibetan border.
2. Martial Sovereign, the title of a Han dynasty ruler, is here a cover name for Emperor Xuanzong.
3. "Men of Qin" are men from the area of the old state of Qin, the capital area "West of the Pass" mentioned four lines later.
4. Lake Koko Nor, Qinghai, or "Blue Sea" in Chinese, on the border between China and Tibet.

On the Border

FIRST SERIES, NINE POEMS

(5-ch., old style; a series of poems written around 750 and dealing with the hardships of peasants recruited into the army and sent to take part in border wars. These are the first, second, fourth, sixth, and ninth in the series.)

7

With heavy hearts we leave the old village,
set out on the long, long road to Jiaohe.[1]
Officials have fixed the date for our arrival—
run away and you're snared in the net of the law!
Ruler, already with such abundance of territory,
why all this opening up of borders?
We turn our backs on love of father and mother,
swallow our sobs, shoulder halberds, and move on.

---

1. The region of Turfan in Xinjiang. The Tang forces were pushing into the area but meeting with strong resistance from Tibetan tribes.

8

Far in the past, that day we left home;
we've outgrown the gibes of fellow recruits.
Not that loved ones are forgotten, our flesh and blood,
but a man never knows when he must die.
We race our horses, slipping the bit from their mouths,
green reins slack in our hands;
galloping down ten-thousand-yard slopes,
hunched in the saddle, we practice how to seize the
enemy flags.

9

We recruits have our commanders to send us off,
but, bound for distant duty, we're people too!
From here we go to face life or death—
no cause for the officers to shout and scowl!
Along the road I happened on someone I knew,
handed him a letter to give to kinfolk:
"Too bad, but we go different ways now,
no longer to share the same hardships and pain."

10

If you draw a bow, draw a strong one,
if you use an arrow, use one that's long.
If you want to shoot a man, shoot his horse first;
if you want to seize the enemy, first seize their leader.
But killing people has limits too;
guarding a state, there're boundaries to be observed.
So long as you manage to keep invaders out—
what point in just seeing how many you can kill?

11

Been in the army ten years and more,
not a single medal to show for it!
Others know how to talk up their exploits—
I could talk too, but I'm ashamed to sound like them!
Fighting on China's central plain,
on top of that, wars with border tribes.
But a brave man faces in all four directions—
how can he beg out when times get hard?

Accompanying Mr. Zheng of the Broad Learning Academy on an Outing to General He's Mountain Villa

TEN POEMS

(5-ch. regulated verse; fifth and ninth in a series of poems written on an outing to the hills south of Chang'an, summer of 752 or 753. On Mr. Zheng, see poem 15.)

12

This stream of yours, as though borrowed from the
 blue Yangzi,
this bit of mountain sliced off from the Jieshi rocks:[1]
green dangling, bamboo shoots broken in the wind;
red splitting open, plums fattened by the rain.
A silver pick to strum the many-stringed zither,
a golden fish exchanged for another round of wine.[2]
We'll move as fancy takes us—don't bother to sweep—
sit wherever we please on the mossy ground.

---

1. A rock formation off the northern coast of China.
2. The golden fish is a bag in the shape of a fish, worn as a girdle ornament by high officials. Someone at the party, presumably General He, has sent the bag to be used in exchange for more wine for the guests.

13

Beside the bed, books piled to the ceiling;
in front of the steps, trees that brush the clouds:
the General has no taste for military matters;
his young sons all are skilled in literature.
Sobering up from wine, we let in the gentle breeze,
listen to poems, pass the quiet night.
Thin summer cloaks are draped on the vines
where cool moonlight, white, shimmers over them.[1]

---

1. Guests have shed their thin cloaks of kudzu fiber and hung them on the vines in the garden.

Ballad of the Beautiful Ladies

(7-ch., old style, around 753; a veiled attack on the Yang family, relatives of Emperor Xuanzong's favorite, Yang Guifei. The gathering centers on her two elder sisters, enfeoffed as the Ladies of Guo and Qin, respectively; the gentleman who arrives later is Yang Guifei's cousin Yang Guozhong, a high minister. The scene is the spring outing held on the third day of the third lunar month at Qujiang, or Winding River, a park in Chang'an.)

14

Third month, third day, in the air a breath of newness;
by Chang'an riverbanks the beautiful ladies crowd,
rich in charms, regal in bearing, well-bred, demure,
with clear sleek complexions, bone and flesh
 well-matched,
in figured gauze robes that shine in the late spring,
worked with golden peacocks, silver unicorns.
On their heads what do they wear?
Kingfisher glinting from hairpins that dangle by
 sidelock borders.
On their backs what do we see?
Pearls that weight the waistband, subtly set off
 the form.
Among them, kin of the lady of cloud curtains,
 pepper-scented halls,[1]
granted titles to the great fiefs of Guo and Qin.
Humps of purple camel proffered from blue caldrons,
platters of crystal spread with slivers of raw fish;
but ivory chopsticks, sated, dip down no more,
and phoenix knives in vain hasten to cut and serve.
Yellow Gate horses ride swiftly, leaving the dust
 unstirred,

bearing from royal kitchens unending rare delights.
Plaintive notes of flute and drum, fit to move the gods,
throngs of guests with their lackeys, all of noblest rank;
and last, another rider with slow and measured stride
dismounts at the tent door, ascends the
  brocade carpet.
The snow of willow catkins blankets the
  white-flowered reeds;
a bluebird flies off, in its bill a crimson kerchief.[2]
Where power is all-surpassing, fingers may be burned.
Take care, draw no closer to His Excellency's glare!

---

1. Yang Guifei, who lived in a palace whose walls were scented with pepper.
2. There were rumors that Yang Guozhong was carrying on an intrigue with the Lady of Guo, and this probably explains the reference to the bluebird, the traditional bearer of love notes. According to Chinese custom, sexual relations between persons of the same surname—in this case between cousins—was considered highly immoral.

Drunken Song (Written for Zheng Qian, Doctor of the Broad Learning Academy)

(5-ch. and 7-ch., old style, 754. Zheng Qian, a close friend of Du Fu, was a distinguished scholar, painter, and poet who, in 750, was appointed to the Broad Learning Academy, though apparently without a very liberal stipend. The "sojourner of Duling" is Du Fu, who at this time was living at Duling in the Chang'an suburbs.)

15

Clomp-clomp, the distinguished gentlemen climb to their high offices;
Dr. Broad Learning in his academy, alone and cold.
Gobble-gobble, in their mansions, weary of fine grain and roasts;
Dr. Broad Learning, not even enough rice to eat.
Doctor with a Way surpassing that of Fu Xi the illustrious,
Doctor with talents to outshine Qu Yuan and Song Yu,[1]
virtue to crown an age, yet always in distress,
fame to hand down ten thousand years, but what good is that?
Out-of-office sojourner of Duling—people all laugh,
coarse garments, skimpy, tight-fitting, sidelocks like floss,
daily at the government granary buying five pecks of rice,[2]
at times off to see his old comrade, Mr. Zheng.
If there's a bit of cash, we look each other up,
spend it buying wine—never doubt that!
We forget formalities, use any language we please;
he's my true teacher in heavy drinking!
As the still night deepens, we pour the spring wine,

before the lamp, fine rain, blossoms falling by the eaves.
We're only aware that in our lofty songs gods and
    spirits join us;
who knows if we'll starve to death, end tumbled in
    a ditch?
Sima Xiangru, of rare talent, with his own hands
    washed the dishes;
Yang Xiong, learned in letters, finally threw himself
    from a tower.[3]
Get busy, my friend, write your "Return";[4]
already your stony fields, your thatched hut grow rank
    with weeds!
The arts of Confucianism, what are they to us?
Confucius and Robber Zhi, both now mere dust!
But why heed such talk, let our thoughts grow gloomy?
While we live and have each other, we'll lift the cup!

---

1. Fu Xi is a mythical ruler of ancient times and a model of virtue. Qu Yuan and Song Yu are renowned poets of the third century B.C.E.
2. A government granary opened in late 753 to relieve people troubled by the unseasonable rains of this and the following year.
3. At one point in his life, the famed poet Sima Xiangru (179–117) ran a wine shop and, leaving his wife to mind the counter, washed the dirty dishes at the community well. The poet, linguist, and official Yang Xiong (53 B.C.E.–18 C.E.), fearful of arrest for political reasons in the time of the usurper Wang Mang, threw himself from the upper story of the office where he was working.

4. When the poet Tao Qian (365–427) quit his official post and returned to private life on his farm, he wrote a prose piece entitled "The Return." Du Fu is urging Zheng Qian to follow Tao's example.

Lamenting Fall Rains

THREE POEMS

(7-ch., old style; second and third poems in the series. In the fall of 754, the Chang'an area was plagued by heavy rains that fell for more than sixty days.. The poems describe the rains and their disastrous effects and hint at the larger troubles facing the nation.)

16

Blusterous winds, unending rains, autumn of chaos,
the four seas, eight directions one solid cloud:
horses going, cows coming, who can make out
  for sure?
Muddy Jing River, clear Wei, how to tell them apart?
From grain tips, ears sprouting, millet heads turned
  black;
no word of how farmers, farmers' wives are faring.
In the city, exchange a bed quilt, get one meager peck
  of grain—
just agree, don't argue over which is worth more!

(The "plain-garbed man" in line 1 is Du Fu, who did not wear the robe of an official at this time but lived in Duling on the outskirts of Chang'an. By this time he was married and had a family.)

17

Plain-garbed man of Chang'an, who takes note of him?
Crude gate closed, he keeps to his country plot.
The father goes nowhere, mugwort and brambles
  grown rampant,
though his little ones, no worries, race around in wind
  and rain.
Rains hiss-hiss, bringing the cold on early;
from the north, wild geese, wings dampened, can
  barely fly on high.
Since start of autumn, not once have we seen the
  white sun.
This earth of ours, muddy, foul—when will it ever dry?

Ballad of Pengya

(5-ch., old style; an account of the journey made by Du Fu and his family in 756 when they fled north from Chang'an to avoid the rebel armies led by An Lushan.)

18

I remember when we first fled the rebels,
hurrying north over dangerous trails;
night deepened on Pengya Road,
the moon shone over White-Water Hills.
A whole family endlessly trudging,
begging without shame from the people we met:
valley birds sang, a jangle of soft voices;
we didn't see a single traveler returning.
The baby girl in her hunger bit me;
fearful that tigers or wolves would hear her cries,
I hugged her to my chest, muffling her mouth,
but she squirmed and wailed louder than before.
The little boy pretended he knew what was happening;
importantly he searched for sour plums to eat.
Ten days, half in rain and thunder,
through mud and slime we pulled each other on.
There was no escaping the rain,
trails slick, clothes wet and clammy;
getting past the hardest places,
a whole day advanced us no more than three or four *li*.
Mountain fruits served for rations,
low-hung branches were our rafter and roof.
Mornings we traveled by rock-bedded streams,
evenings camped in mists that closed in the sky.

We stopped a little while at the marsh of Tongjia,
thinking to go out by Luzi Pass;
an old friend there, Sun Zai,
ideals higher than the piled-up clouds;
he came out to meet us as dusk turned to darkness,
called for torches, opening gate after gate,
heated water to wash our feet,
cut strips of paper to call back our souls.[1]
Then his wife and children came;
seeing us, their tears fell in streams.
My little chicks had gone sound to sleep;
he called them to wake up and eat from his plate,
said he would make a vow with me,
the two of us to be brothers forever.
At last he cleared the room where we sat,
wished us goodnight, all he had at our command.
Who is willing, in the hard, bleak times,
to break open, lay bear his innermost heart?
Parting from you, a year of months has rounded,
Tartar tribes still plotting evil,
and I think how it would be to have strong wings
that would carry me away, set me down before you.

---

1. Reference to an ancient rite used to call back the souls of travelers when they have been dispersed by fright. Commentators disagree whether in this case the rite was actually performed, or whether the allusion to it here is merely figurative.

Pitying the Prince

(7-ch., old style; written in the autumn of 756, when Du Fu was detained in Chang'an by the rebel forces. In the sixth month of this year, the rebels seized the city, looting and massacring many of the inhabitants, including members of the imperial family who had failed to escape in time. The white-headed crows in line 1 are omens of evil. Greeting Autumn Gate is the western gate by which Emperor Xuanzong and his entourage fled the city.)

19

Over Chang'an city walls white-headed crows
fly by night, crying above Greeting Autumn Gate.
Then they turn to homes of the populace, pecking at
great mansions,
mansions where high officials scramble to flee
the barbarians.
Golden whips broken, royal steeds dropping dead,
even flesh and blood of the ruler can't all get away
in time.
How pathetic—costly disc of green coral at his waist,
this young prince standing weeping by the roadside!
I ask, but he won't tell me his name or surname,
says only that he's tired and in trouble, begs me to
make him my servant.
A hundred days now, hiding in brambles and thorns,
not a spot on his body where the flesh is untorn.
Sons and grandsons of the founder all have
high-arched noses;
heirs of the Dragon line naturally differ from
plain people.
"Wild cats and wolves in the city, dragons in the wilds,
prince, take care of this body worth a thousand in gold!

I dare not talk for long, here at the crossroads,
but for your sake, prince, I stay a moment longer.
Last night, east winds blew rank with the smell of blood,
from the east came camels crowding the old Capital.[1]
Those Shuofang troops, good men all—
why so keen, so brave in the past, so ineffectual now?[2]
I've heard the Son of Heaven has relinquished his throne,
but in the north his sacred virtue has won the Uighur
khan to our side.[3]
The Uighurs slash their faces, beg to wipe out
our disgrace.
Take care, say nothing of this—others wait in ambush!
I pity you, my prince—take care, do nothing rash!
Auspicious signs over the five imperial graves never
for a moment cease."[4]

---

1. The rebel army used camels for transport. Chang'an is called the "old Capital" because the emperor no longer resides there.
2. Reference to the troops in the Ordos region north of Chang'an, who had earlier fought successfully against the Tibetans but in 756 suffered a disastrous defeat at the hands of the rebel armies of An Lushan.
3. Emperor Xuanzong's son and successor, Emperor Suzong, succeeded in enlisting the help of the Uighur khan and his troops in the struggle against the rebels. As a mark of their sincerity, the Uighurs slashed their faces when they vowed to aid the Chinese ruler.
4. The speaker is hinting that the Tang imperial line is not yet destined to come to an end. On auspicious signs over the imperial graves, see poem 23.

Moonlight Night

(5-ch. regulated verse; written in 756 when Du Fu was being held captive in Chang'an. His wife and family were in Fuzhou to the north.)

20

From her room in Fuzhou tonight,
all alone she watches the moon.
Far away, I grieve that her children
can't understand why she thinks of Chang'an.
Fragrant mist in her cloud hair damp,
clear lucence on her jade arms cold—
when will we lean by chamber curtains
and let it light the two of us, our tear stains dried?

Facing Snow

(5-ch. regulated verse; written late in 756, after the government forces had made an unsuccessful attempt to retake Chang'an from the rebel forces and suffered a disastrous defeat. The districts mentioned in line 7 are where Du Fu's family had taken refuge.)

21

On the battlefield wailing, so many new ghosts;
fashioning his poem of sorrow, lonely old man.
Ragged clouds press down in the fading twilight;
swift snow dances in the turning wind.
Gourd dipper discarded, no more green of wine in
  the cask;
stove beside me, still a flicker of red.
From nearby districts all word cut off,
grieving, I sit writing words in the empty air.

Spring Prospect

(5-ch. regulated verse; written early in 757 when Du Fu was still a captive in Chang'an.)

22

The nation shattered, mountains and rivers remain;
city in spring, grass and trees burgeoning.
Feeling the times, blossoms draw tears;
hating separation, birds alarm the heart.
Beacon fires three months in succession,
a letter from home worth ten thousand in gold.
White hairs, fewer for the scratching,
soon too few to hold a hairpin up.[1]

---

1. Men wore hairpins to keep their caps in place.

Passing Zhaoling Again

(5-ch. *pailü*; Zhaoling was the mausoleum of Emperor Taizong (r. 627–48), the second ruler of the Tang and the one largely responsible for founding the dynasty. The first eight lines describe his rise to power. The five-hued clouds of the last line are an auspicious omen appearing in response to Taizong's greatness. The poem was written in 757, when the dynasty's fortunes seemed anything but glorious.)

23
From rude darkness the heroes rose;
amid songs of praise, destiny chose him;
in wind and dust, his three-foot sword,
armor donned for the altars of the land;
wings to his father, pure in civil virtue;
heir of the great charge, wielder of war's might;
his holy vision wide and huge as heaven,
in service of the ancestors more radiant than the sun.
The mound-side chamber lies wrapped in
    empty slopes;
warriors, bearlike, guard the blue-green hill.
Once more I gaze up the pine and cypress road,
watching five-hued clouds drift by.

Dayun Temple, Abbot Zan's Room

FOUR POEMS

(5-ch., old style; Dayun Temple was in the southwestern sector of Chang'an. The poems were probably written in 757 while Du Fu was being held captive by the rebel government in Chang'an, his moves carefully watched in case he tried to escape to the loyalist forces, as in fact he did later in the year. Abbot Zan's full name is unknown.)

24

My mind in a realm of pure crystal,
clothes dampening in springtime rain,
I walk slowly through a succession of gateways,
to the inner garden and its sequestered meeting.
Doors open and close just as I reach them,
a bell strikes, hour for the monks' meal.
This ghee gives lasting nourishment to innate nature,
this food and drink support a faltering body.
Many days the Abbot and I've been arm-in-arm
   companions,
speaking our mind without timid evasions.
Yellow warblers traverse the rafters,
purple doves fly down from eave guards.
I've chanced on a spot that suits me exactly,
strolling among blossoms as slowly as I please.
And to lift my spirits, Tang Xiu here
smiles, urging me to write a poem.[1]

---

1. Tang Huixiu was a Buddhist monk of the fifth century famous for his literary accomplishments. Du Fu here uses the name to refer to Abbot Zan.

25

Shoes of thin-spun soft green silk,
fine white headcloth, sparkling bright,
carefully stored away as provisions for elder clergy,
brought out now for the likes of me!
I see myself as a man devoid of charm,
but in our dealings I'm still his new-found friend,
this Daolin whose talents outshine the age,
this Huiyuan who in virtue surpasses all others.
Showers drench the bamboo by twilight eaves,
wind blows over the cresses by the spring well.
As skies darken I confront the murals,
most conscious of the damp from dragon scales.[1]

---

1. Zhi Daolin (314–366) and Huiyuan (334–417) were eminent Buddhist monks to whom Du Fu likens Abbot Zan. Dayun Temple was famous for the murals in its various halls and pagodas, some of which Du Fu is viewing in the last couplet and which no doubt included paintings of dragons. The dragon here perhaps symbolizes Emperor Xuanzong, under whom Du Fu served before his capture by the rebels, the "damp" representing the imperial favor he enjoyed then.

26

Lamp glow lights my sleeplessness;
mind clear, I breathe a wondrous fragrance.
As night deepens, the main hall looms larger than ever;
wind, stirring, sets the eave bells chiming.
Skies are black, blotting out the springtime court;
earth's cleanness houses hidden perfumes.
The Jade Rope, revolving, breaks in two and vanishes;
the iron phoenix seems ready to fly quietly away.[1]
Sanskrit now and then sounds from the temple;
the toll of the bell lingers, echoing round my bed.
Come morning, as I go home through fertile fields,
I'll hate to see the yellow of their dust and sand.[2]

---

1. "Jade Rope" refers to two stars in the Big Dipper, which appear to break apart as they sink behind the temple roof. The phoenix is an iron weather vane fixed to the roof. In the line that follows, the monks are chanting the morning service.
2. Probably a reference to the rebel forces occupying the capital.

27

The boy draws dawn water from the well,
the bucket with practiced swiftness rising to his hand,
sprinkles drops without soaking the ground,
sweeps in such a way you can't tell he's used a broom.
Sunrise hues illumine the storied buildings;
fog, melting, lifts from high windows.
Leaning from both sides, blossoms arch the pathway;
willow fronds, gently swaying, dangle to the terrace.
But now I'm pressed by irksome worldly cares;
good times of retirement must come later.
We've met and talked, our deepest hearts in accord;
how can they gag us into total silence?
Tendering good-byes, I set off on my return;
we must part for a time: I look back in longing.
Deep sloughs of mud wait to soil us;
yap! yap!—many dogs in our city.[1]
I can't break loose from bonds and fetters,
but, chance permitting, I'll rest here again from
    my trials.
Your presence, Abbot, is like white snow—
I no longer fear to take hold of what's hot.[2]

1. References to the unsavory political climate of the time.
2. An allusion to *Book of Odes*, poem 257: "For who can take hold of something hot / without first moistening his hand?" That is, Abbot Zan helps to "cool" the poet's worries and vexations.

Thinking of My Little Boy

(5-ch. regulated verse, 757; Du Fu in Chang'an, thinking of his younger son, who was with his wife in Fuzhou. The boy's nickname was Jizi, or Pony Boy, Ji being the name of a famous horse of ancient times. "Discoursing" in line 4 is facetious, since the boy was only four years old at this time. Lines 5 and 6 describe the scene in Fuzhou.)

28

Pony Boy—spring and you're still far away;
warblers sing, so many in this warmth.
Parted, I'm startled at how the seasons change.
My bright boy, with whom is he discoursing?
Valley stream, a road over empty hills,
rustic gate, village of old trees—
Thinking of you, sorrowing, all I do is doze,
back to the sun, hunched over on the bright veranda.

A Letter from Home

(5-ch. *pailü*; written in the fall of 757, when Du Fu was a Reminder at the court of Emperor Suzong in Fengxiang. "Home" is where Du Fu's wife and children were living in Fuzhou. He had not heard from them for over ten months.)

29

I sent mine off, entrusted to a passing traveler;
he came back bringing me this letter from home!
Today I learn the true state of affairs
in that village, not ours, though home from
some time past.
Bear Cub—luckily no problems there;
Pony Boy—he's the one I miss most![1]
Confronting old age, my life rootless, lonely,
grieving at the times, so seldom we meet;
hair half gray, I race around curtained halls,
fill my one assignment, attend the ruler's
belled carriage.
Chang'an's northern gates rank with evil vapors;
here in the western suburbs, white dew newly fallen,[2]
cool winds, wild geese beginning their migrations,
autumn rains—many fish will be spawned.[3]
A farmer's life in those empty hills—
I long to be there at last, shouldering a hoe!

---

1. Bear Cub is the childhood name of Du Fu's elder son Zongwen; Pony Boy is his second son Zongwu.

2. Chang'an at this time was in the hands of the rebel forces. "Western suburbs" refers to Fengxiang west of the capital where Emperor Suzong had his court.
3. Both wild geese and fish are associated in Chinese lore with letters because of tales of letters tied to the feet of wild geese or delivered in the belly of a fish.

Jade Flower Palace

(5-ch., old style; a description of a detached palace built west of Chang'an in 647. Occupied briefly by Emperor Taizong, it was later made into a Buddhist temple and then abandoned. By the time Du Fu viewed it in 757, it had fallen into ruin.)

30

Valley stream tortuous, pine winds unending,
gray rats scurry under ancient tiles—
who knows what ruler's dwelling,
by sheer cliffs built and then abandoned?
In north-facing chambers, the green of ghostly fires,
ruined walkways, sad waters lapping them:
nature's ten thousand pipings are its true flutes now,
autumn colors its emblazonment.
Beautiful women gone to yellow dust,
long gone the powder and mascara that
  adorned them,
years past attending their lord in his golden carriage—
of those lost ones, only stone horses remain.[1]
When sorrow comes, sit on the grass,
sing loud songs, drench your palm in tears.
On and on the journey ahead—
who lives for long?

---

1. Stone figures ornamenting a grave mound.

Qiang Village

THREE POEMS

(5-ch., old style; written in the fall of 757 when Du Fu, having incurred the anger of Emperor Suzong because of his defense of the high official Fang Guan, was ordered to return to the village of Qiang in Fuzhou where his wife and children were staying. The poems depict his reunion with his family after an absence of a year or more.)

31

Red clouds, their towering shapes move westward;
sun's rays streak down to the level plain.
Bramble gate, sparrows and little birds chattering—
the traveler home from his thousand-mile trek!
My wife, amazed to see me alive,
recovers from her astonishment, wipes away tears.
A world in chaos, buffeted, tumbled,
by sheerest chance I've managed to make it back.
Faces of neighbors crowd the wall;
pitying, they add their sighs and exclamations.
As night deepens, we bring out candles,
face one another as though in a dream.

32

Along in years, barely managing to stay alive,
I came home to find pleasures few.
My dear boy won't let go my knees,
afraid I'll go off and leave him again.
I remember times gone by, hunting for a cool spot,
how we threaded among the pondside trees.
But now north winds howl and bluster;
wherever I turn, a hundred cares to needle me.
So good to know the grain's been harvested,
to hear the wine trickling from the lees.
For now at least, enough to dip from,
to ease me in my declining years.

33

Our chickens start in squawking wildly—
the arrival of visitors sets them squabbling.
I shoo them into the trees, then for the first time
hear the knocking at my rustic gate;
four or five village elders
come to ask about my long absence, my long
  trip home.
Each carries something in his hand;
from tilted casks, muddy wine, and clear,
profuse apologies for the wine's poor flavor:
"No one these days to work the millet fields,
wars and uprisings that never end,
all the young ones off to the eastern campaign."
I ask if I may sing them a song,
sign of my deep gratitude in these troublesome times.
Song ended, I gaze upward with a sigh,
from those on four sides, tears streaming down.

Spring Night's Stay in the Left Office

(5-ch. regulated verse; 758, when Du Fu was a Reminder in the Left Office, or Imperial Chancellery. In the third couplet he is listening for the sound of palace doors being unlocked and imagining he hears the horse bells of officials arrived at court.)

34

Blossoms shadowy, twilight on palace walls;
chatter-chatter, nest-bound birds fly by.
Stars loom above, their light wavering over ten
 thousand doorways;
the moon swells in brightness as it climbs the
 upper sky.
Sleepless, I listen for the sound of bronze locks,
in the wind imagine I hear jeweled horse bells.
I've sealed papers to present to the Throne at dawn;
again and again I ask the hour of the night.

The Man with No Family to Take Leave of

(5-ch., old style; Tianbao in the first line refers to the outbreak of the An Lushan rebellion in the fourteenth year of the Tianbao era, 755.)

35

Ever since Tianbao, silence and desolation,
fields and sheds mere masses of pigweed and bramble.
My village, a hundred households or more,
in these troubled times scattered east and west,
not a word from those still living,
the dead all gone to dust and mire.
I was on the side that lost the battle,[1]
came home, looked for the old paths,
so long on the road, to find empty lanes,
sun grown feeble, pain and sorrow in the air.
All I meet are foxes and raccoon dogs;
fur on end, they snarl at me in anger.
For neighbors on four sides who do I have?
One or two aging widows.
But the roosting bird loves his old branch;
how reject it, narrow perch though it is?
Come spring, I shoulder the hoe alone,
in evening sun, once more pour water on the fields.
Local officials know I'm back;
they call me in, order me to practice the big drum.[2]
Maybe they'll assign me to duty in this province—
but still I've no wife, no one to take my hand.
Posted nearby, I'm one man all alone;
sent to a far-off assignment, more lost than ever.

But house and village a wilderness now,
near or far are all one to me.
And always I grieve for my mother, sick so long,
five years left buried in a mere ditch of a grave.
She bore me, but I hadn't the strength to care for her;
to the end, both of us breathed bitter sighs.
A living man, but no family to take leave of—
how can you call me a proper human being?

---

1. The defeat of the imperial forces at Xiangzhou in the third month of 759.
2. The drum used in battle to signal troop movements.

An Old One Takes His Leave

(5-ch., old style; the poem shifts back and forth between monologue and description.)

36

In four directions, no peace, no safety—
how can an old one rest easy?
Sons, grandsons all lost in battle,
what use to keep this one body alive?
He throws his stick aside, goes out the gate,
comrades looking on in pity and concern.
Luckily I still have my teeth,
though alas, little sap left in these bones!
But I'll put on armor like a proper fellow,
give my long salute, take leave of the commander.
His old wife slumps by the roadside weeping,
year-end, in nothing but an unlined robe.
Who knows, perhaps their final parting;
he thinks how she'll suffer from the cold.
Once gone, likely he'll never return,
yet he hears her begging him, "Eat well!"
Fortifications at Tumen hold firm,
the ford at Xingyuan well guarded;
different from the way it was at Yecheng—[1]
though we die in the end, time's on our side now.
Life has its meetings and partings;
what difference, in your prime or your dotage?
But, remembering days when he was young,
he holds back, hesitant, then gives a long sigh.

From ten thousand regions they're off to combat;
beacon fires top the hills and knolls.
Grass and trees reek with piled up corpses,
streams of blood redden the rivers and plains.
What village is a happy land now?
How can I go on dawdling?
I'll quit my thatch-roofed home, be off,
though the pain of it strikes my vitals!

---

1. Where the imperial forces suffered a severe defeat at the hands of the rebels in 759.

Presented to Gao Shiyan

(5-ch. regulated verse; date uncertain. Gao Shiyan was a nephew of the poet Gao Shi (716–765) and a member of the group of poets, which included Li Bai, with whom Du Fu spent time in his youth in Henan. These are the "long-ago companions," all facing hardship now, about whom he reminisces.)

37

Where was it we parted last,
to meet again, now both old men,
our long-ago companions luckless as ever,
hiding our traces, alike in hardship and care?
Friends to talk literature with—since I lost them
I waste time acquainting myself with the wine
seller's stall.
Pent-up ambitions cherished for a lifetime,
seeing you, come back to me—no way to stop them!

The Official of Stone Moat

(5-ch., old style, 759; Shihao, or Stone Moat, was a village in Henan that Du Fu passed through in the course of his travels. The official is searching for people who can be impressed into military service.)

38

At evening I put up at Stone Moat Village;
that night an official came to round up people.
The old man at the inn scaled the wall and ran away;
the old woman came to open the gate.
The official, how fiercely he shouted!
The old woman, how pitiful her cries!
Then I heard her say to him,
"Three sons sent to defend Yecheng—[1]
a letter came from one of them,
the other two lost in the fighting.
One alive, no more than a borrowed life,
dead ones gone for all time!
Here in the house not another soul,
only a grandchild, still nursing at the breast.
His mother stays to look after him,
indoors or out, barely a skirt to cover her.
I'm an old woman, little strength left,
but let me go with you tonight.
If you're pressed for hands at Heyang,
at least I could cook the morning rations."
Late that night no more sound of people talking,
but I thought I heard weeping and muffled sobs.
At dawn when I set out once more,
only the old man to see me off.

---

1. On the defeat at Yecheng, see poem 36.

Presented to Wei Ba, Gentleman in Retirement

(5-ch., old style, around 759; nothing is known about Wei Ba, though the designation Ba, or "Eighth," indicates he was eighth in seniority among his male siblings and cousins.)

39

Life is not made for meetings;
like stars at opposite ends of the sky we move.
What night is it, then, tonight,
when we can share the light of this lamp?
Youth—how long did it last?
The two of us grayheaded now,
we ask about old friends—half are ghosts;
cries of unbelief stab the heart.
Who would have thought?—twenty years
and once again I enter your house.
You weren't married when I left you;
now suddenly a whole row of boys and girls!
Merrily they greet their father's friend,
ask me what places I've been.
Before I finish answering,
you send the boys to set out wine and a meal,
spring scallions cut in night rain,
new cooked rice mixed with yellow millet.
Meetings are rare enough, you say;
pour the wine till we've downed ten cups!
But ten cups do not make me drunk;
your steadfast love is what moves me now.
Tomorrow hills and ranges will part us,
the wide world coming between us again.

Lovely Lady

(5-ch., old style, around 759; a description of a woman whose family has been wiped out in the rebellion and whose husband has deserted her.)

40

Lovely lady, fairest of the time,
hiding away in an empty valley;
daughter of a good house, she said,
fallen now among grasses of the wood.
"There was tumult and death within the passes then;
my brothers, old and young, all killed.
Office, position—what help were they?
I couldn't even gather up my brothers' bones!
The world despises you when your luck is down;
all I had went with the turn of the flame.
My husband was a fickle fellow,
his new girl as fair as jade.
Blossoms that close at dusk keep faith with the hour,
mandarin ducks will not rest apart;
but he could only see the new one laughing,
never hear the former one's tears—"
Within the mountain the stream runs clear;
out of the mountain it turns to mud.
Her maid returns from selling a pearl,
braids vines to mend their roof of thatch.
The lady picks a flower but does not put it in her hair,
gathers juniper berries, sometimes a handful.
When the sky is cold, in thin azure sleeves,
at dusk she stands leaning by the tall bamboo.

Qinzhou

TWENTY MISCELLANEOUS POEMS

(5-ch. regulated verse. In the fall of 759, escaping famine, Du Fu journeyed with his family west to Qinzhou in Gansu on the upper reaches of the Wei River. The following are the first, second, fourth, thirteenth, and eighteenth in the series.)

41

Everywhere I look, the sorrow of human existence:
certain persons aiding me, I set out on a distant
 journey,
with labored slowness cross Long Pass in terror,
come this far, engulfed in borderland gloom.
Waters low, nights on Fish Dragon River;
hills uninhabited, autumn on Bird and Rat Mountain.
Heading west, I ask about wartime beacons,
spirit downcast, lingering, halting here.

(Wei Xiao was a warlord who flourished in the Qinzhou area in the first century. The Wei River was noted for its clear waters.)

42

Temple north of Qinzhou's walls,
famed site of Wei Xiao's palace:
temple gates old, coated in moss and lichens;
in the fields, a hall painted red and green, deserted.
The moon illumines dewdrops dangling from
    the leaves,
clouds tag after winds that sweep the valley.
The clear Wei, most heartless of all,
in my time of sorrow flowing east without me.

(Drums and horns are used in military action; here they are indicative of the unrest in the western border region due to invasions by Tibetan and Uighur tribes.)

43

Drums and horns in borderland counties
as night falls over the river plain,
in the autumn air I hear them rending the earth;
scattered on the wind, mournfully they fade among
the clouds.
The cold cicada clings to its leaf in silence,
the lone bird slowly returns to its mountain.
Ten thousand directions caught up in this one sound;
my road—in the end where will it take me?

44

South Rampart Temple on the hilltop,
by a stream called North Flowing Spring;
old trees stand in an empty garden,
channel sending clear water down to the whole village.
Autumn flowers at the foot of steep rocks,
evening shadows beside the sleeping bell.[1]
I gaze around, grieve for myself and for the times;
valley winds for my sake make moaning sounds.

---

1. The bell, fallen from its frame, lies on its side on the ground.

45

In this far-off land, autumn almost over,
mountains lofty, a traveler not yet gone home;
outpost clouds forever breaking, meshing,
borderland sun that sheds only feeble rays.
Tense times, beacon fires continually signal alarms;
again and again orders come to mobilize the troops.
These western tribes kin in marriage to our Sovereign,
how dare they defy Heaven's majesty![1]

---

1. The Tang emperors had twice sent an imperial princess to be the bride of a Tibetan ruler, but in Du Fu's time the Tibetans defied the Son of Heaven by raiding China's western borders.

New Moon

(5-ch. regulated verse; in Qinzhou. The River of Heaven is the Milky Way.)

46

Frail rays of the crescent newly risen,
slanting beams only a fraction of the full circle,
barely lifted above the old fort,
already hidden in slivers of evening cloud.
Stars of the River of Heaven keep their hue unchanged,
barrier mountains, untouched, cold as before.
In the courtyard white dew forms,
moisture imperceptibly drenching the
chrysanthemums.

The Cricket

(5-ch. regulated verse; in Qinzhou.)

47
Cricket, so tiny, so lowly,
why do your sad notes move us so?
Among the grass roots you cry inconsolably,
under the bed, wanting companionship now.
Can the traveler, long on the road, hold back his tears?
Can the abandoned wife endure the hours till dawn?
Plaintive strings, shrill piping of woodwinds,
never stir us as do Nature's sounds!

View over the Plain

(5-ch. regulated verse; in Qinzhou.)

48

Clear autumn, no end to the view,
layers of darkness beginning to pile up:
the distant river blends its purity with the sky;
a solitary fortress shrouded in deep mist.
Trees all but leafless, the wind strips them further;
mountains far off, sun just sunk beyond.
Lone crane, why so long going home,
the groves already thick with crows?

Off on a Long Journey

(5-ch. regulated verse; in Qinzhou. Though the poem seems to deal with the departure of a friend, some commentators take it as descriptive of Du Fu's own departure on his western journey.)

49

Now when the armor-clad fill heaven and earth,
why off on a distant journey?
Close friends done with their moment of tears,
the saddled horse sets out from the lone, walled town.
Grass, trees of the waning year,
borderland river shining in frost and snow:
it seems only yesterday we parted—
I know now how he felt, that man of old.[1]

---

1. Reference to a poem on parting by Jiang Yan (443–504), the lines: "It seems like yesterday I saw you off, / dew already soaking the ground before the blinds."

Empty Moneybag

(5-ch. regulated verse; in Qinzhou. Du Fu speaks in a humorous vein.)

50

Fruit of the azure oak, bitter but edible,
dawn mists, high up, but one can dine on them.[1]
Others all bumble along somehow—
why is my way such a tangle of woes?
Nothing on the stove, the well at dawn frozen,
no decent clothing, bed at night so cold;
but an empty moneybag—that shame I dread,
so I cling to this lone copper coin.

---

1. Azure oak acorns and the rosy mists of dawn were said to be the food of immortal spirits.

Staying Overnight in Abbot Zan's Rooms

(5-ch. regulated verse; 759. A note appended by the poet says: "Zan was the head priest of Dayun Temple in the capital but has been banished to this place." Both Du Fu and Abbot Zan had been associates of the high minister Fang Guan, who was removed from office and exiled to a provincial post in 758. Abbot Zan had perhaps been exiled from Chang'an because of this association. The word Long in the last line is a general name for the area of Gansu where Qinzhou was located.)

51

When did you come here with your
pewter-ringed staff,
autumn winds already blowing shrill?
Rains have spoiled the chrysanthemums in the
inner courtyard,
frost has toppled lotuses on half the pond.
Banished, but how does that harm innate nature?
In this emptiness you never depart from Zen.
Now we've met, we can stay a night together,
a Long moon looking down on us roundly.

On a Moonlit Night, Thinking of My Younger Brothers

(5-ch. regulated verse; in Qinzhou.)

52

Martial drums cut off all human concourse;
borderland autumn, cry of a lone wild goose.[1]
Tonight we enter the season of white dew,
though the moon still shines with a homeland
  brightness.
I've younger brothers, every one of them scattered,
no home where I can ask if they're dead or alive.
I send letters that never succeed in getting through,
much less now, with hostilities unceasing!

---

1. According to legend, the wild goose is the bearer of letters to distant places.

Taking Leave of Abbot Zan

(5-ch., old style; written in the fall of 759 when Du Fu, after only four months in Qinzhou, left in search of food.)

53

The hundred rivers each day flow eastward,
the traveler, never at rest, moves on.
My life, bitter with fruitless wanderings—
when will they find an end?
Reverend Zan, elder in Buddha's teachings,
banished here from the capital,
here to suffer more worldly trials,
face gaunt and lined with care.
One morning a willow branch in hand,
then already the beans have ripened twice.[1]
These our bodies, drifting clouds:
north, south, how limit the direction they'll take?
In a strange district I come on an old friend,
with newfound delight pour out my feelings.
Sky endless, borderlands cold,
the year running out, dogged by chill and hunger;
wind from the plain buffets my traveling clothes,
I prepare to say good-bye as twilight approaches.
The horse neighs, remembering his old stall;
homing birds have finished folding their wings.
Places we used to gather long ago
in a day or two become weeds and brambles!
We look at each other, bent with age,
one going, one left behind—both must eat hearty!

1. "Willow branch" perhaps refers to the time in the previous year when Du Fu and Abbot Zan parted in Chang'an, since willow branches are a symbol of parting. The lines are obscure though, and there are other interpretations.

Leaving Qinzhou

(5-ch., old style; written in late 759 when Du Fu left Qinzhou and headed for Tonggu, "the source of the Han" River, because he had heard that food was plentiful there.)

54

I'm getting old—stupid, listless,
can't seem to plan my course in life.
Nothing to eat, I ask after the "happy land";[1]
no clothes, I dream of southern climes.
At the source of the Han, tenth month and on,
they say the weather's like bracing autumn,
grass and trees not yet yellowed or stripped,
mountains and waters more wonderful still.
Chestnut Pavilion—a most auspicious name!
Surely rich farmlands must surround it,
lots of wild yams to fill the belly,
honeycombs in the cliffs, easy to gather,
thick-groved bamboo sending up winter shoots,
clear ponds just right for boating.
True, there's the hardship of a lengthy journey,
but hopefully I'll find outings I've always longed for.
This place straddles a major highway,
fearful bustle of people coming and going,
but I don't mix in such matters—not my nature,
and its hill and stream outings don't ease my cares.
In its streambeds, no precious stones;
its garrison fields yield only meager harvest.
What is here to solace an old man?
Disillusioned, I've no wish to stay any longer.

Sun's hues hidden behind the lone outpost,
crows cawing, massed on the town walls;
at midnight I set off by wagon,
water my horse in cold embankment streams.
Stars and moon strewn high above,
chance stragglings of cloud and mist;
so huge the compass of heaven and earth,
so long the road I travel!

---

1. The land of plenty that the distressed peasants long for in poem 113 of the *Book of Odes*.

Red Valley

(5-ch., old style; farther along on the journey described in the preceding poem.)

55

Cold skies thick with frost and snow,
but the traveler must move on,
sad, though the year's end approaches,
no prospect I'll ever come this way again.
At dawn I set off from Red Valley station,
steep perilous roads from this point on,
a jumble of stones, but no other cart track to follow—
I've already greased the axles well.
Deep mountains, strong wind to make the
  going harder,
come nightfall my little ones are hungry;
spirits flag, village so far off,
its smoke in sight, but how to get there?
Poor, ailing, more destitute than ever,
no use to think of homeland now.
Always I fear I'll die by the roadside,
forever a laughingstock for men of high ideals.[1]

---

1. By "men of high ideals," Du Fu probably has in mind the recluses of Chinese lore, who never attempted, as did Du Fu, to take part in political life.

Seven Songs Written During the Qianyuan Era (758–60) While Staying at Tonggu District

(7-ch., old style; poems recording Du Fu's experiences in 759 when, fleeing from famine, he led his family west to Tonggu in Gansu. Zimei is Du Fu's courtesy name.)

56

A traveler, a traveler, Zimei his name,
white hair tousled, dangling below the ears,
through the years I gather acorns in the wake of the
monkey pack:
cold skies at dusk within a mountain valley.
No word from the middle plain, no hope of
going home;
hands and feet chilled and chapped, skin and flesh
grown numb.
Ah-ah, song the first, song already sad;
mournful winds for my sake come down from the sky.

57

Long hoe, long hoe, handle of white wood,
I trust my life to you—you must save me now!
No shoots of wild taro where mountain snows
   drift high;[1]
robe so short, pull as I may it won't hide my shins.
So with you I go empty-handed home;
the boys grumble, the girls whine, my four walls
   are still.
Ah-ah, song the second, the song at last breaks free;
village lanes for my sake put on the face of pity.

---

1. Or, following another version of the text, "shoots of wild lily," used in medicine.

(Du Fu had four brothers; the youngest was with him in Tonggu, the others living in the east.)

58

I have brothers, younger brothers in a place far away,
three of them sickly, not one of them strong;
parted in life, to veer and turn, never to meet;
barbarian dust blackens the sky, the road is long.
Wild geese fly east, behind them the cranes—
if they could only carry me to your side!
Ah-ah, song the third, the singer's third refrain;
if I should die here, how would you find my bones?

(Zhongli is in Anhui, south of the Huai River.)

59

I have a sister, little sister, living in Zhongli,
husband dead these many years, her orphaned ones
  still young.
On the long Huai, waves leap up, dragons and
  serpents rage;
we haven't met for ten years—when will you come?
I want to go in a little boat, but arrows fill my eyes;
far away in that southern land, banners of war abound.
Ah-ah, song the fourth, four times I've sung;
forest monkeys for my sake wail even at noon.

60

Mountains on four sides, high winds, canyon
waters swift;
cold rain sloshes down, bare trees wet with it.
Yellow mugwort over old town walls, clouds that
never part,
white foxes leaping, yellow foxes that stand still:
why has my life brought me to this forsaken valley?
I get up in the night, sit, ten thousand cares
crowding around.
Ah-ah, song the fifth, song long continuing—
I can't call back my wandering soul, gone to its
old home.

(Clearly a political allegory, though commentators do not agree on what the dragon and the vipers stand for.)

61

To the south lives a dragon in a mountain pool
where old trees, dark and lush, touch limb to
  bending limb.
When tree leaves yellow and fall, he goes to his
  winter sleep,
and from the east come vipers to play on the
  waters there.
Passing by, I marveled that they would dare
  come forth,
drew a sword to slash them, but put it up again.
Ah-ah, song the sixth, its purpose long denied;
stream-cut valley, for my sake, put on spring clothes
  again!

62

Born a man, gained no fame, body already old,
three years fleeing hunger over harsh mountain roads.
Young men are the lords and statesmen of
Chang'an now;
riches, high position—grab them while you're young!
Here in the mountains a scholar, friend from old times;
all our talk is of the past, painful to recall.
Ah-ah, song the seventh—hush, leave off singing!
Look up at the heavens as the bright sun hurries by.

Dreaming of Li Bai

(5-ch., old style; written in 759 when Li Bai was in exile in the south, the first of two poems.)

63

Parting from the dead, I've stifled my sobs,
but this parting from the living brings constant pain.
South of the Yangzi, land of plague and fever—
no word comes from the exile.
Yet my old friend entered my dreams,
proof of how long I've pined for him.
He didn't look the way he used to,
road so far, farther than I can guess.
His spirit came from where maple groves are green,
then went back, left me in borderland darkness.
Now you're caught in the meshes of the law;
how could you have wings to fly with?
The sinking moon floods the rafters of my room
and still I seem to see it lighting your face.
Where you go, waters are deep, waves so wide,
don't let the dragons, the horned dragons harm you!

Departing Tonggu District

(5-ch., old style; written in the last month of 759 when Du Fu left Tonggu for Chengdu.)

64

The worthy man never blackens his stove,
the sage never warms his sitting mat.[1]
And I, a hungry, stupid man,
what hopes for a settled home?
When I first arrived in this mountain region,
I halted my cart, delighted in its remoteness.
But troubles keep pushing me onward—
four journeys in a single year![2]
In sadness I leave these far-off parts,
set out again on the long, long road.
I rested my horse by clouds of Dragon Tarn,
turned my head toward the rocks of Tiger Scarp,[3]
and now at the crossroads take leave of a few friends,
clasp their hands, tears again flowing.
Our friendship's not an old one,
but what heartbreak for this old man!
In life's affairs inept and clumsy,
then to have hit on a refuge like this!
To go, to stay—neither could please me;
the contentment of the woodland birds puts me
  to shame.

---

1. It is said that the ancient philosopher Mozi never used a stove long enough to blacken it because he was so busy hurrying about the country preaching against warfare and promoting his ideas on universal love. Confucius was said never to have sat still long enough to warm his sitting mat because he was similarly untiring in his efforts to alleviate the ills of society.
2. From Luoyang, where he had gone at the end of the previous year, to Huazhou, Huazhou to Qinzhou, Qinzhou to Tonggu, and now Tonggu to Chengdu.
3. Places in the Tonggu area.

Moving In

(7-ch. regulated verse; written in the spring of 760 when Du Fu moved into his newly built "thatched hall" at Wanhuaqi, or Wash-Flower Stream, west of Chengdu.)

65

On western waters of Wash-Flower Stream,
the owner has built his house in the seclusion of
 wooded banks,
certain that beyond city walls troublesome affairs are
 few,
that clear river water can wash away a traveler's cares.
Countless dragonflies dart in unison high and low,
a pair of mandarin ducks dive and bob side by side.
If I took a notion, I could voyage ten thousand miles,
eastward in a little boat headed for the coast.[1]

---

1. Du Fu's new home was near Ten-Thousand-Mile Bridge on the Jin, or Brocade, River, another name for Wash-Flower Stream. The bridge was so called because it was said that "A ten-thousand-mile journey [eastward down the Yangzi] begins here."

River Village

(7-ch. regulated verse; in Chengdu.)

66

One bend of the clear river crooks the village in its
flow;
long summer days, river village, all activity stilled.
Swallows from the bridge come and go as they please,
gulls on the water friendlier, more fearless than ever.
My aging wife rules a sheet of paper, fashioning us
a chessboard;
the boys hammer a needle, making it into a fishhook.
With all these ailments, all I require is medicine;[1]
of humble station, what more could I ask?

---

1. "I've an old friend who supplies me with rations of rice;" is an alternate reading given in one version of the text.

Old Country Fellow

(7-ch. regulated verse; in Chengdu. The "old country fellow" is Du Fu. The painted horns in the last line are bugles used in the army camps, a reminder of the unstable condition of the times.)

67

Old country fellow in front of his hedge where the river
bank rounds,
bramble gate not properly oriented but faced so it
gives on the river.
Fishermen's nets cluster in deep pools of clear water,
peddlers' boats return with rays of the setting sun.
Always on my mind, the long road, sorrows of
Sword Gate;[1]
a wisp of cloud—why, I wonder?—hovers over
Zither Terrace.[2]
Royal armies have yet to report recovery of the
eastern districts;
autumn comes to Chengdu city, painted horns, their
mournful sound.

---

1. The long road that separates Du Fu from his homeland in the east; Sword Gate is a difficult pass that he crossed on his way from Qinzhou to Chengdu.
2. Zither Terrace is the grave of the poet Sima Xiangru (179–117 B.C.E.), a native of Chengdu, which was situated near Du Fu's house. Sima Xiangru was famous for his playing of the *qin*, or zither.

Hating Separation

(7-ch. regulated verse; in Chengdu. Luoyang is the region where Du Fu was born and grew up.)

68

Once parted from Luoyang, four, five thousand miles;
five, six years now, far-off barbarian riders swooping
down on us.
Grass and trees wither and fade, a journeyer beyond
Sword Gate;
war pikes bar my path, by riverside I grow old.
Recalling home, I pace the moonlight, stand in the
clear evening;
thinking of younger brothers, watching clouds, at
midday half asleep.
I hear that in Heyang these days our troops pile victory
on victory.
Quick now, Commander, capture You and Yan for us![1]

---

1. Heyang is the province of Henan south of the Yellow River where the government forces defeated the rebel leader Shi Siming in 760. You and Yan are the regions in the northeast around Beijing where the rebels had their stronghold. The Commander is Li Guangbi, leader of the government troops.

A Guest Arrives

(7-ch. regulated verse; in Chengdu.)

69

North of my lodge, south of my lodge, everywhere
spring rivers;
day by day all I see are flocks of gulls converging.
Flower paths never before swept for a guest,
my thatch gate, opening for you, opens for the first
time.
For food—the market's far—no wealth of flavors;
for wine—my house is poor—only old muddy brew.[1]
If you don't mind drinking with the old man next door,
I'll call across the hedge, and we'll finish off what's left.

---

1. "Muddy brew" refers to a rice wine of milky consistency, usually home-brewed.

Spring Night, Delighting in Rain

(5-ch. regulated verse; in Chengdu, the "City of Brocade.")

70

The good rain knows when to fall,
stirring new growth the moment spring arrives.
Wind-borne, it steals softly into the night,
nourishing, enriching, delicate, and soundless.
Country paths black as the clouds above them;
on a river boat a lone torch flares.
Come dawn we'll see a landscape moist and pink,
blossoms heavy over the City of Brocade.

Jueju Composed at Random

NINE POEMS

(7-ch. *jueju*; in Chengdu; the first, second, fourth, sixth, seventh, and eighth in the series.)

71

Anyone knows a traveler's grief never can be dispelled,
yet these heedless spring colors descend on my
 river pavilion!
Enough that blossoms open in inordinate haste,
but why make the warblers chime in with so
 much chatter?

72

Peaches, damsons I planted by hand, in no
 way ownerless;
my hedge, low as it is, surrounds a proper dwelling.
Why then are spring winds bent on robbing me,
blowing in the night, breaking down these
 flowering branches?

73

Second month spent by now, third month arrives;
old age creeps up, how many more springs will I see?
But cease thinking of endless matters beyond my ken—
first let me drink up the cups allowed me in this life!

74

So lazy I never even venture beyond the village;
sun still high, I call my son to close the bramble gate.
Emerald moss, muddy wine, all silent here in the woods;
blue water, spring breeze, dusk over fields beyond.

75

Willow fluff along the path spreads a white carpet;
lotus leaves dot the stream, plating it with green coins.
By bamboo roots, tender shoots where no one
    sees them;
on the sand, baby ducks asleep beside their mother.

76

West of my lodge, lithe mulberries, leaves ready
 for picking;
by the riverbank, slim, slim, thin stalks of wheat.
How long our life?—spring already gone to summer.
Never neglect this fragrant brew, flavor sweet
 as honey!

Visiting Xiujue Temple

(5-ch. regulated verse; written in the spring of 761, in Chengdu, where Xiujue-si, or the Temple for Cultivating Enlightenment, was located.)

77
Country temple, river and sky widespreading;
mountain doors hidden in blossoms and bamboo.
The gods must be helping out my poetry,
granting me a spring excursion like this!
Stones along the pathway join in twisted strands,
clouds on the river linger or press on.
Zen branches offer roost for whole flocks of birds,
but at twilight the drifter goes home in sorrow.[1]

---

1. Zen branches are simply branches of trees in the temple grounds, but here the Buddhist term Chan, or Zen, which literally means "meditation," suggests the calm and safety of temple life, a life denied to Du Fu, "the drifter."

Second Visit

(5-ch. regulated verse; 761 in Chengdu, from a second outing to the Temple for Cultivating Enlightenment.)

78

I recall the temple, visited before,
bridge welcomely familiar as I cross it again.
River and mountains seem to be expecting me,
blossoms and willows perfect in their indifference.[1]
Fields are lush, veiled in thin mist,
sands warm, sunlight lingering over them.
The traveler's sorrows are wholly banished now—
where else but here would I go?

---

1. The blossoms and willows neither welcome nor repel the visitor but display the "egoless" attitude appropriate to a Buddhist temple.

On the Spur of the Moment

(7-ch. regulated verse; 761.)

79

River slopes, already midmonth of spring;
under the blossoms, bright mornings again.
I look up, eager to watch the birds;
turn my head, answering what I took for a call.
Reading books, I skip the hard parts;
faced with wine, I keep my cup filled.
These days I've gotten to know the old man of Emei.[1]
He understand this idleness that is my true nature.

---

1. Emei is a famous mountain southwest of Chengdu.

River Pavilion

(5-ch. regulated verse; in Chengdu. The "river pavilion" was a small kiosk in Du Fu's garden.)

80

I lie on my back, river pavilion warmth,
intone poems, gaze out over the fields.
Flowing water—my mind doesn't try to keep up;
lingering clouds—my thoughts match their slowness.
Silently, silently, spring about to end;
joyful, joyful, each thing in its own nature.
Can't go home to my old woods yet—
to battle gloom I make myself write poems.

Song: How My Thatch Roof Was Blown Away by Autumn Winds

(7-ch. and irregular lines, old style; in Chengdu.)

81

Eighth month, midautumn, fierce winds howl
    and bluster,
strip away three layers of thatch from my roof!
Thatch blown over the river, plastered on river fields,
snagged high up in tips of the tall grove;
low down, whirling, tumbling, sunk in the
    swampy pond.
Gangs of boys from the village to the south—they
    think I'm old and helpless—
brazenly steal the thatch right before my eyes,
bundle it up in plain sight, make off into the bamboo!
Shout till lips are dry, mouth parched, it does no good!
Back home I lean on my stick, grumble to myself.
After a while, winds abating, clouds ink-colored,
autumn sky, wide, vacant, darkens into evening.
Cloth quilt chilly as iron, so many years in use—
my children, bad sleepers, have torn the lining with
    their feet.
Where the bed is, leaks in the roof, not a dry spot,
raindrops thick as hemp seedlings, never letting up.
Since the troubles landed on me, I don't sleep much.
Long night wet and clammy—how to make it to dawn?
Where can I get a big broad shelter a thousand, ten
    thousand spans wide,

huge roof that all the world's poor people can share
with smiling faces?
Wind and rain won't budge it, solid as a mountain—
Ah-ah, when I can see that roof soaring before my eyes,
my one hut blown away, my freezing to death—none
of that will matter!

Meetingplace of a Hundred Woes: A Ballad

(7-ch., old style; in Chengdu.)

82

I remember when I was fifteen, still a child at heart,
healthy as a yellow calf racing all around.
Eighth month in the garden, pears and jujubes ripe;
in one day I shinnied up the trees a thousand times.
Now suddenly fifty years old,
much sitting, lying down, little walking or standing.
I make myself use smiling words speaking to my hosts[1]
but see with sorrow that my whole life is a
    meetingplace of a hundred woes.
Go in the door: as usual, four bare walls;
my old wife eyes me with a face just like mine,
while my foolish children, no respect for their father,
howl outside the kitchen door, demanding to be fed.

---

1. The friends in Chengdu who helped him meet his daily needs.

Journeyer's Pavilion

(5-ch. regulated verse; 762. In the summer of this year, rebellion broke out in Chengdu, and Du Fu fled to nearby Zizhou.)

83

Autumn window still colored by dawn,
bare trees, high winds that go on blowing:
sun comes up beyond cold mountains,
river flows through last night's mist.
In times of good government, no one unused;[1]
frail, sickly, I'm an old man now.
How much of life left me,
vagrant, tumbleweed rolled around by the wind?

---

1. An allusion to *Laozi*, sec. 27: "The sage is always good at rescuing others; hence no one is unused."

Crossing Guanglu Pass

(7-ch. regulated verse; on the way to Zizhou.)

84

Mountain journey, sunset, down the steep escarpment,
far to the south a thousand mountains, ten
  thousand reddening.
Hour when birds in the branches chatter raucously;
twilight shadows, no one but the lone traveler.
Though my horse may shy, no fear I'll plunge into
  deep ravines,
only, when grasses stir, terror of the long bows
  of bandits.
How to bring back again that Kaiyuan era?[1]
Roads these days—so many blocks and perils!

---

1. The years 713–41, Du Fu's youth, when the empire was peaceful and well governed, and roads were safe to travel.

Visiting the Temple of Abbot Wen

(5-ch., old style; probably written in 762 when Du Fu was in Zizhou. The identity of Abbot Wen is unknown.)

85

Country temple hidden in giant trees,
mountain monks living high and low on the slope,
stone gates, sunlight a different color,
red mists trailing this way and that.
Pushing deeper, I start up the windy stairway,
long creepers tangled, coiling, uncoiling.
In the forecourt a fierce tiger crouches;
only then do I reach Reverend Wen's lodge.[1]
I peer down at the town of ten thousand houses,
its smoke and grime beyond the flight of steps.
Ten years and more, except to preach,
the Master's never been down the mountain.[2]
Rich men donated their gold;
in his hall of worship he's splendidly serene,
a great pearl free of fleck or blemish,
a bright moon that hangs in empty air.
Du Fu's a man now south, now north,
snarled in undergrowth seldom mowed.
For long now I've been tainted by poetry and wine,
somehow acquired the badge and garb of office.
But marquises and mole crickets alike
in the end go to the graveyard.
I long to hear of that Prime Principle,
to begin the first stage of mind cultivation.

With your golden scalpel cut the film from my eyes—
it will be worth more to me than a hundred gems.
With the Law of no-birth draw me upward,
perhaps with your help to reach that Truth.[3]

---

1. The tiger is clearly intended to symbolize Abbot Wen's spiritual power and attainment, though whether we are meant to see it as a live animal, a stone figure, or simply a figure of speech, I cannot say.
2. The word translated as "preach" is literally *yuhua*, "to rain flowers," a reference to the story of how the heavens rained down flowers when the famous Chinese monk Fayun (467–529) preached on the Lotus Sutra.
3. The image in line 25 of the skilled physician using a golden scalpel to cut the film of ignorance from the eyes of his patient derives from the Nirvana Sutra. "No-birth" refers to the ultimate reality of all things, which, as the Heart Sutra states, is characterized by "no birth, no cessation, no impurity, no purity."

Distant View of the Temple on Ox Head

(5-ch. regulated verse; Zizhou, in the spring of 763.)

86

I see Crane Forest Temple on Ox Head,
path laddering up to it, threading deep shade.
Colors of spring float beyond the mountain;
the Milky Way sleeps in the shadow of the main hall.
Its lamp of doctrine never for a day has ceased shining,
its ground paved with alms of yellow gold.
I should give up being an old man who sings
  crazy songs,
aim instead for a mind of no-attachment.[1]

---

1. The state of Buddhist enlightenment. Crane Forest in the first line is an allusion to the death of Shakyamuni Buddha, when the two *sal* trees between which he was lying burst into white blossoms in their sorrow so that they resembled trees where white cranes were roosting.

On Hearing That Government Forces Have Recovered Henan and Hebei

(7-ch. regulated verse; Zizhou, early 763, when Du Fu received word that the government forces had at last recovered control of the areas north and south of the Yellow River, areas that had been overrun by the rebel armies. Du Fu imagines how he will journey down the Yangzi to his home in Luoyang. Unfortunately, the journey never materialized.)

87

Beyond Sword Gate suddenly word—Jibei recovered![1]
On first hearing it, tears splash all over my robe.
I look at my wife and children—what worries now?
hastily bundle up my books, mad with delight.
White-haired, singing wild songs, all the wine I want,
in green spring the whole family going back home,
straight off through Ba Rapids, threading Wu Rapids,
then down to Xiangyang, heading for Luoyang!

---

1. The northern part of the ancient province of Jizhou, stronghold of the rebels.

Letting the Boat Drift

(5-ch. regulated verse; 763, when the poet had gone to Cangqi, or Green Stream District, to see off a friend and was traveling down the Jialing River.)

88

Green Stream District, seeing off a traveler,
mountains icy, rain that never clears.
Fearful that a mounted horse might slip,
I return instead by river-borne boat.
Green—I hate to see the peaks go by so swiftly;
yellow—I know that oranges and citrons are on the way.
In the river's flow, what magnificent freedom!
I sit in silence as delights amble by.

Ascending the Tower

(7-ch. regulated verse; 764, in Chengdu. Like Wordsworth's "London, 1802" ("Milton! thou shouldst be living at this hour"), this poem revolves around the longing for a great man of the past, though he is never actually named. Jinjiang, or Brocade River, runs through Chengdu; Yulei, or Jade Rampart, is a mountain northwest of the city. In the previous year, forces invading from Tibet in the west had seized the Tang capital, Chang'an, though the Chinese armies quickly regained control of the city. Du Fu, climbing a tower and looking out over the troubled land, laments these threats to the reigning dynasty and recalls the career of Zhuge Liang (181–234), hero of the Three Kingdoms period, who came to the aid of Liu Chan, the Last Ruler of the kingdom of Shu, which had its capital at Chengdu. The tombs of the Last Ruler and Zhuge Liang were located in Chengdu. The Liangfu Song was a ballad that Zhuge Liang frequently sang in his younger days.)

89

Tall tower, blossoms pressing close—you wound the
journeyer's heart;
troubles in ten thousand quarters, I climb and
look down.
Brocade River, hues of spring spread over heaven and
earth;
Jade Rampart, drifting clouds transform it, now as
long ago.
The dynasty, our North Star, never to be undone—
marauders of the western mountains, cease your
incursions!
Moved, I recall that even the Last Ruler has his
ancestral temple.
At close of day I intone the Liangfu Song.

Jueju
FOUR POEMS

(7-ch. *jueju*, third in a set of four; 764, in Chengdu.)

90

A pair of yellow warblers sing in the green willow,
a file of white herons climb the blue sky.
Framed in my window, the thousand autumn snows of
  the western peaks;
tied by my gate, a boat to take me ten thousand miles
  east to Wu.

Broken Boat

(5-ch., old style; written in 764 when Du Fu returned to his "thatched hall" in Chengdu after having fled for a time because of local rebellion. "Rivers and lakes" in the first line refers to the lower Yangzi valley where Du Fu wandered in his youth and, by extention, to an area of peace and freedom from worldly cares.)

91

All my life a heart set on rivers and lakes,
long ago got my little boat ready,
not meaning it just for clear streams here,
daily outings by my brushwood gate.
Then trouble and chaos, fleeing rebel troops,
all the time longing for these old hills.
Now I find neighbors are no more,
only wild bamboo that grows taller and taller.
My boat—gunwales I'll never thump again—
sunk in water a whole autumn by now.
Looking up, I see birds winging west;
look down, shamed by the river's eastward flow.
Old boat—possibly I could raise it,
or easily enough find a new one.
What pains me is having to run away so often.
Even a simple hut I can't stay in for long!

Recalling the Past

(7-ch., old style, second of two poems with this title; 764, when Du Fu had been assigned a post as military adviser under the governor general of Chengdu.)

92

I recall the past, Kaiyuan's days of splendor,
when even little towns boasted ten thousand
households,
rice grains like liquid lard, glutinous rice white,
public and private granaries alike full to overflowing.
Roads of all nine ancient provinces free of bandits;
starting on distant journeys, no one bothered about a
"lucky" day.
Qi silks, Lu white silk, carload on carload;
men plowed, women tended silkworms, each in
proper season;
in the palace the sage ruler, soothed by sacred music,
throughout the empire, comrades forever faithful
and true.
A hundred years and more, no calamities, no upheavals,
rites and music of Shusun Tong, laws of Xiao He.[1]
Who then heard of a bolt of silk costing ten
thousand cash?
But fields sown in grain flow now with blood,
Luoyang's palaces burned to the ground,
in new steps of ancestral temples, foxes and
rabbits burrow.
I dare not ask the old people, so painful to hear,
fearful they'll recite again their tales of rebellion.

I, a paltry subject, stupid, ineffectual,
enrolled among the court officials, recipient of a
  stipend—
Our Sovereign—like Xuan of Zhou, may he renew the
  nation's fortunes![2]
Old, ailing, my tears flow into the Yangzi and the Han.

---

1. Shusun Tong and Xiao He were statesmen of the early Han dynasty who fashioned fitting rituals and legal codes for the empire.

2. King Xuan (r. 827–781 B.C.E.), by means of his wise rule, drove back the foreign tribes threatening China and renewed the waning fortunes of the Zhou dynasty.

Two *Jueju*

(5-ch. *jueju*; probably written around 764 in Chengdu. In line 3 the swallows are gathering mud to build their nests.)

93

In late sun, the beauty of river and hill;
on spring wind, fragrance of flower and grass:
where mud is soft the swallows fly,
where sands are warm, mandarin ducks doze.

94

River cerulean, birds whiter against it;
mountains green, blossoms about to flame:
as I watch, this spring too passes—
what year will I ever go home?

Restless Night

(5-ch. regulated verse; 764.)

95
Cool of bamboo invades my room,
moonlight from the fields fills the corners of the court;
dew gathers till it falls in drops;
a scattering of stars, now there, now gone.
A firefly threading the darkness makes its own light;
birds at rest on the water call to one another;
all these lie within the shadow of the sword—
powerless I grieve as the clear night passes.

Night Duty at the Government Office

(7-ch. regulated verse; 764, in Chengdu.)

96

Clear autumn, government office, by the well a
  paulownia tree cold;
river town, alone on night duty, candles burning low:
bugle sounds in the long night—downcast, I talk
  to myself;
overhead, the moon's brilliance—fine, but who looks
  at it?
War's ceaseless dust and tumult, no letters
  getting through;
border outpost desolation, roads impassable—
after ten years enduring the poorest of luck
I force myself to rest here on this one branch.[1]

---

1. Reference to *Zhuangzi*, ch. 1: "When the tailorbird builds her nest in the deep wood, she uses no more than one branch."

Sitting Alone

(5-ch. regulated verse; 764, in Chengdu.)

97

Saddened by autumn, white head turning,
propped on a cane, lone city at my back:
river waters have fallen, shoals and banks exposed,
skies empty, landscape crisp and clear.
Old age cheats me of blue-wave wanderings;
against lifelong inclinations I put on the red badge
 of office.
Looking up, I envy birds in the yellow dusk,
bound for their forest on light-feathered wings.

Spring Day, River Village

(5-ch. regulated verse, fourth in a set of five poems with this title; 765, in Chengdu. In the first month of this year Du Fu resigned his official post because of poor health and returned to private life in his thatched hall.)

98

Aided in infirmity, I dangled the red badge;
retired, back home, I stroll over purple moss.
Behind suburban gates, I plan for old age;
in goverment halls the wealth of talent put me
  to shame.
Beyond the swallows, heat haze spirals up;
where the gulls are, leaves of water plants unfurl.
My neighbors send me fish and turtles
and come quite often to ask how I am.

Leaving Shu

(5-ch. regulated verse; written in the fifth month of 765 when Du Fu left Chengdu, the main city of the Shu region, intending to journey down the Yangzi to the east.)

99

Five years a sojourner in the district of Shu,
one year spent in Zizhou;
why stay cooped up in this border outpost?
I'll break away, be off to Xiao and Xiang excursions![1]
All hopes ended, hair gone gray,
for the years left, I'll go with the white gulls.
The nation's safety or peril—leave that to the
  great statesmen.
Why must I go on shedding tears forever?

---

1. Xiao and Xiang are rivers, in the region south of Lake Dongting in Hunan, noted for their natural beauty.

A Traveler at Night Writes His Thoughts

(5-ch. regulated verse; 765.)

100

Delicate grasses, faint wind on the bank;
stark mast, a lone night boat:
stars hang down, over broad fields sweeping;
the moon boils up, on the great river flowing.
Fame—how can my writings win me that?
Office—age and sickness have brought it to an end.
Fluttering, fluttering, where is my likeness?
Sky and earth and one sandy gull.

On the Spur of the Moment

(7-ch. *jueju*; 766, when the poet was traveling down the Yangzi from Yun'an to Kuizhou. The third watch is the period around midnight.)

101

River moon barely a foot or two away from us;
a windblown torch lights the night, nearly third watch.
Along the sand, roosting herons bunched
together, silent;
by the stern a fish leaps up, comes down with a smack.

Ballad of the Firewood Vendors

(7-ch., old style; 766, describing local customs in Kuizhou, an area of steep hillsides along the Yangzi.)

102

Kuizhou women, hair half gray,
forty, fifty, and still no husbands;
since the ravages of rebellion, harder than ever
  to marry—
a whole life steeped in bitterness and long sighs.
Local custom decrees that men sit, women stand;
men mind the house door, women go out and work,
at eighteen, nineteen, off peddling firewood,
with money they get from firewood, making
  ends meet.
Till they're old, hair in two buns dangling to the neck,
stuck with wild flowers, a mountain leaf, a silver pin,
they struggle up the steep paths, flock to the
  market gate,
risk their lives for extra gain by dipping from salt wells.
Faces powdered, heads adorned, sometimes a trace
  of tears,
cramped fields, thin clothing, the weariness of
  stony slopes—
But if you say all are ugly as the women of Witch's
  Mountain,
how to account for Zhaojun, born in a village to
  the north?[1]

1. Wushan, or Witch's Mountain, was on the Yangzi near Kuizhou. Wang Zhaojun was a court lady of Han times, famous for her beauty, who came from a village near Kuizhou.

On the River

(5-ch. regulated verse; in Kuizhou. Jing-Chu is an old name for the area along the Yangzi where Kuizhou was situated.)

103

On the river, day after day so much rain—
dreay, desolate, the Jing-Chu autumn.
High winds strip the leaves from the trees;
through the long night I hug my marten-fur coat.
Political accomplishments? I stare at the mirror.
Wisdom in conduct? Alone, I lean from an upper floor.
In these perilous times, how to repay my Sovereign?
Old and frail, I can't stop thinking of it.

Late Sunshine

(7-ch. regulated verse; in Kuizhou. A palace of the king of the ancient kingdom of Chu was said to have been situated at the foot of Witch's Mountain east of Kuizhou. White Emperor City was a rocky fortress built by a warlord of the first century C.E. on the site that later became the city of Kuizhou.)

104

North of the Chu king's palace, yellow twilight;
west of White Emperor City, traces of passing rain:
late sunlight floods the river, shimmers over
  rocky scarps;
returning clouds envelop the trees, swallow up the
  mountain village.
Lung trouble in my declining years—I sleep on a
  high pillow;
remote outpost, worrisome times—I close my
  gate early.
In this bandit-ridden region, can't stay for long;
here in the south, truly, a soul waiting to be recalled.[1]

---

1. Du Fu is referring to the "Summons to the Soul," a poem written to call back the departed soul of the exiled poet and statesman Qu Yuan (third century B.C.E.), who drowned himself in a river in the region of Chu, and is hinting that it is time that he himself be recalled to the capital.

Midnight

(5-ch. regulated verse; 766, in Kuizhou. The "western lodge" was a two-story building situated at the top of a steep cliff where Du Fu lived for a time, apparently some kind of guest house for officials.)

105

Western lodge atop a hundred-span height;
at midnight I pace by gauze window curtains:
a shooting star arcs the river, whitening the water;
the setting moon bathes the sands in empty glow.
Hidden birds, I know, are in their chosen trees;
I picture huge fish that lurk beneath the waves.
I've kin and friends enough to fill the world,
but in this time of arms and armor, few letters
  get through.

They Say You're Staying in a Mountain Temple

(5-ch. regulated verse, second of two poems; written in 766 when Du Fu was in Kuizhou on the upper Yangzi, the Yangzi-Han region mentioned in the poem. His younger brother Feng was in the seacoast area south of the Yangzi delta. Du Fu had one older brother, who apparently died early, and four younger brothers [actually, half brothers]. Counting all the brothers, Feng was the fifth.)

106

My fifth brother Feng is alone in the region east of the Yangzi, and for three or four years I have had no word from him. I am looking for someone to take him these two poems.

They say you're staying in a mountain temple,
in Hangzhou—or is it Yuezhou?
The wind and grime of war so long have kept us parted!
In Yangzi-Han, bright autumns waste away.
While my shadow rests by monkey-loud trees,
my soul whirls off to where shell-born towers rise.[1]
Next year on floods of spring I'll go downriver,
to the white clouds at the end of the east I'll look
  for you!

---

1. Towerlike mirages at sea, believed to be formed by the breath of mollusks.

Night

(7-ch. regulated verse; 766, in Kuizhou.)

107

Dew has fallen, a tall sky, clear autumn air;
empty hills, solitary night, the traveler's spirits prone
  to alarm:
a dim lamp lights it, lone sailboat moored till morning;
new moon still hangs on the horizon, a pair of fulling
  mallets pounding.[1]
Southern chrysanthemums—again I encounter them,
  laid up by sickness this time;
no letters from the north—the wild goose has no pity.[2]
I stroll by the eaves, lean on my cane, gaze at
  the Herdboy;[3]
far in the distance the Milky Way must reach to the
  Emperor's city!

---

1. Fulling mallets are used to soften cloth and spread its fibers when women cut and sew clothes for winter.
2. The previous year Du Fu had seen the blooming of the southern chrysanthemums in Yun'an, farther upstream on the Yangzi. In Chinese lore the wild goose is the bearer of letters.
3. The Herdboy is the star Altair. According to legend, the Herdboy fell in love with the Weaving Girl, the star Vega. They were married, but after her marriage the Weaving Girl neglected her weaving. Her father punished the couple by

moving the Weaving Girl to the opposite side of the Milky Way and decreeing that they meet only once a year, on the night of the seventh day of the seventh month, when friendly magpies form a bridge for them over the River of Heaven, or Milky Way.

Zongwu's Birthday

(5-ch., old style. Zongwu, nicknamed Pony Boy (see poem 28), was Du Fu's second son; he was probably about fourteen at this time. The "decrepit one" is Du Fu himself.)

108

Young boy, when did we first see you?
On this day deep in autumn you were born.
Ever since you learned the speech of the capital,
your name's been paired with that of your old father!
Poetry is our family undertaking—
the world is taking note of how you do.
Study diligently the principles of the *Wenxuan*;
never mind cavorting in gaudy colored clothes.[1]
Decrepit one, they're putting out the seating mats,
but you're so tottery you can't sit up in your seat.
Now let the fine wine flow, to each his portion,
tip the jar slowly, pouring drop by drop.

---

1. The *Wenxuan*, or *Literary Anthology*, a lengthy compendium of prose and poetry compiled by Xiao Tong (501–531) of the Liang dynasty, was regarded as the foundation of a literary education. The next line is a reference to the philosopher Lao Laizi who, though an old man, continued to dress in bright children's clothing and play in the presence of his parents, that they might forget their own advanced age.

Autumn Meditations

EIGHT POEMS

(7-ch. regulated verse, a set of eight poems; written in Kuizhou in the fall of 766. The poems deal with the coming of autumn—always a time of sadness in Chinese literature—the local scene, Du Fu's memories of the capital as it was before the rebellion led to its destruction, the perils facing the nation, and the poet's own old age, declining health, and failure to achieve anything of significance in political life. The first three poems focus mainly on the Kuizhou scene, while the latter five center around Du Fu's memories of Chang'an, though the two locales are often fused within a single poem. Cast in the highly demanding seven-character regulated verse form, the poems are considered by many to be among the greatest works of classical Chinese poetry, though due to their allusive and often mysterious language, they seem to defy satisfactory translation.)

109

Icy dew withers and scars the maple groves;
Witch's Mountain, Witch's Gorge, bleak with
  autumn's chill;
on the river, waves leap up to join the sky;
above the outpost, windblown clouds blanket the
  earth in darkness.
Clumps of chrysanthemums open again—tears for
  days now gone;
lone boat moored by a single strand—my heart in the
  gardens of home.
Cold-month clothes everywhere urging speed with
  ruler and scissors;
high above White Emperor City, the swift pounding of
  evening mallets.

110

Setting sun angles over Kuizhou's lone walls;
Big Dipper my guide, I gaze far off toward the
  shining capital.
I hear gibbons cry three times, and in truth tears
  come down;[1]
charged with a mission, vainly I boarded the
  eighth-month raft.[2]
Picture-hung ministry, its incense remote from the
  pillow I lie on;[3]
mountain towers, their white-daubed parapets
  dimmed with plaintive flutes.
Look there! Moonlight on vines and creepers that cloak
  the rocks—
already it shines on the rush and reed blossoms of the
  river shoals.

---

1. An old song says that hearing three cries from the gibbons of the Yangzi gorges will invariably move one to tears.
2. A double reference to the story of how the explorer Zhang Qian, on a mission for Emperor Wu of the Han, set out by raft and traced the Yellow River to its source; and to a story of how a man living by the sea boarded a raft that appeared in the eighth month and took him to the River of Heaven,

the Milky Way. Both journeys led to success, whereas Du Fu's official career ended in failure.

3. Du Fu is recalling times when he was an official in the Department of State Affairs, whose walls were decorated with portraits of distinguished men. Women attendants burned incense to perfume the robes of officials spending the night on duty at the ministry.

111

Mountain-walled, a thousand houses, stillness of
morning sun:
day after day in my river tower I sit in midslope blue.
Two nights running, fishermen's boats still bob-
bobbing on the water;
clear autumn, yet the swallows keep on darting,
darting to and fro.
Like Kuang Heng, I submitted my memorial, won scant
merit or fame,
like Liu Xiang, passed on the classics, results hardly
what I'd hoped for.[1]
Fellows I went to school with, most of them now far
from poor;
in the five tomb towns, wearing light furs, they ride
their fat horses.[2]

---

1. Kuang Heng and Liu Xiang were Han period officials who won imperial favor through the memorials they submitted or their labors in collating classical texts, in Liu Xiang's case handing on his duties to his son, Liu Xin. But the memorial Du Fu submitted on behalf of Fang Guan merely roused the emperor's ire, and his efforts to win a position he could pass on to his son ended in failure.

2. The five tomb towns were suburbs of Chang'an that grew up around the tombs of five Han emperors and were peopled in Tang times by wealthy or influential families. The line alludes to a passage in *Analects* VI, 4, that speaks disparagingly of an official who went about "wearing light furs and drawn by fat horses."

112

I've heard them say, Chang'an's like a chessboard;
sad beyond bearing, the happenings of these
  hundred years![1]
Mansions of peers and princes, all with new
  owners now;
in civil or martial cap and garb, not the same as before.
Over mountain passes, due north, gongs and
  drums resound;
wagons and horses pressing west speed the
  feather-decked dispatches.[2]
Fish and dragons sunk in sleep, autumn rivers cold;
old homeland, those peaceful times, forever in
  my thoughts!

---

1. As in a game of chess, Chang'an was seized in 756 by An Lushan's rebel troops, retaken by the government forces the following year, seized by Tibetan invaders in 763, and retaken by the Chinese in the same year.
2. The first line of the couplet refers to measures taken to block the Uighur invasions from the north, the second, to troops sent west to repel the Tibetans. Feathers were attached to military dispatches to indicate the need for rapid delivery.

113

Gates of Penglai Palace look toward the southern
mountains;
the dew-catcher's golden shaft cleaves the night sky.[1]
Far to the west the Queen Mother descends by
Jasper Lake;
purple emanations come from the east, flooding
Hangu Pass.[2]
Like clouds parting, pheasant-tailed screens unfold;
dragon scales bathed in sun, we behold the august
countenance.[3]
I, who lie beside the vast river, startled at the
waning year,
how often by blue-patterned doors have I heard the
call to morning audience!

---

1. Penglai, a palace of Chang'an in Han times, was named after the mythic island in the eastern sea where immortal spirits were said to live. In Chang'an, Emperor Wu of the Han erected a colossal statue with a pan in its hand for collecting night dew. The dew was believed to grant long life to anyone drinking it. Du Fu uses Han dynasty terms to refer indirectly to Emperor Xuanzong and his Daoist-inspired search for longevity.

2. More Daoist allusions. The Queen Mother of the West was an immortal who feasted an ancient Chinese ruler at Jasper Lake, in the Kunlun Mountains west of China, and later descended from the sky to instruct Emperor Wu of the Han in the arts of longevity. When the sage Laozi, coming from the east, approached the Hangu Pass, his arrival was signaled by purple emanations. The keeper of the pass, realizing that the sage was about to leave China, asked him to write a book, whereupon Laozi wrote the Daoist classic that bears his name.
3. Du Fu is recalling his days as an official in Chang'an, when he attended dawn audiences with the emperor. The emperor, wearing robes figured with dragon designs, sat behind screens ornamented with pheasant tail feathers, which opened at the time of the audience. The last line refers to the doors of the throne room, decorated in a blue-lacquered chain pattern.

114

Mouth of Qutang Gorge, Winding River Park:
ten thousand miles of wind and haze couple them in
pale autumn.[1]
Corridors of Flower Calyx Hall imbued with the
imperial aura;
the little Hibiscus Garden, invaded by frontier woes.[2]
Pearl-sewn blinds, embroidered columns, surround the
yellow swans;
brocade hawsers, ivory masts, startle the white gulls.[3]
I turn my head, mourning for those sites of song
and dance,
land of Qin, from ancient times, province of emperors
and kings.

---

1. The mouth of the Qutang Gorge of the Yangzi was just west of Kuizhou. Winding River was a park in Chang'an (see poem 14).

2. Flower Calyx was a hall in the Xingqing Palace in Chang'an frequented by the emperor. The corridors led to the Hibiscus Garden in Winding River Park. The second line of the couplet might be interpreted as meaning that the garden has been invaded by frontier soldiers of the An Lushan rebellion, or it might mean that memories of the garden fill the poet's sad thoughts as he resides in the frontier region of Kuizhou.

3. These lines depict the palaces of the Tang rulers, with beautiful blinds and columns encircling an inner lake where pleasure boats with ivory-decorated masts moved among water birds.

115

Kunming Lake, work project of Han times,
yet before my very eyes, Emperor Wu's flags
and banners![1]
Weaving Girl, loom threads idle in the
evening moonlight;
stone whale, scales and carapace wobbling in
the autumn wind.[2]
Waves float wild rice grains, blackening the
sunken clouds;
dew chills the lotus calyx, its spilled pollen red.
From this border outpost to the end of the sky, a road
only birds can travel.
Here where rivers and lakes strew the earth, one
old fisherman.

---

1. Kunming Lake, just west of Chang'an, was constructed by Emperor Wu of the Han and used for training his ships in naval warfare; the flags are those of the ships. Once again Du Fu is using Han period allusions to refer to Tang times.
2. On the edge of Kunming Lake stood a statue of the mythic Weaving Girl (see poem 107). In the waters of the lake was a stone whale that was said to roar and waggle its flippers and tail in stormy weather. The whale seems to have been of a somewhat peculiar kind.

116

Kunwu, Yusu, a twisty, winding way;
Purple Tower Peak, its shady side cast in Meipi Pond.[1]
Fragrant rice: peck, leave behind, parrots, grains;
emerald parasol tree: nest, grow old,
  phoenixes, branches.[2]
Picking greens with a lovely lady, we talk together in
  the spring,
with immortals in the same boat, set out again
  at evening.[3]
Once my gaudy writing brush stirred the
  very elements;
now I drone, gaze into the distance, white head
  bitterly bowed.

---

1. Kunwu is a region south of Chang'an, Yusu a river in the region; Purple Tower Peak is in the Southern Mountains, south of the capital near Meipi Pond. Du Fu is recalling outings in the capital area.
2. The words are scrambled for poetic effect; normal word order would be: Parrots peck, leave behind grains of fragrant rice; phoenixes nest, grow old in branches of the emerald parasol tree.

3. Commentators suggest various allusions that may be relevant, though none of them make clear just what the lines are about. Possibly, they refer to Du Fu's memories of his days in Chang'an.

Dispelling Gloom

(7-ch. *jueju,* a series of twelve poems on various themes; 766, in Kuizhou. This is the first in the series.)

117

Thatched cottage, brushwood door, houses strewn
  like stars;
waves curl up, the river darkens, first flying drops
  of rain.
Wild birds lead their chicks, feed them by mouth with
  red berries;
valley women collect my money, leave me white fish
  in return.

Drunk, I Fell Off My Horse; Friends Came to See Me, Bringing Wine

(7-ch., old style; in Kuizhou.)

118

Du Fu, aging guest of the governor,
done drinking, singing songs, brandishing a
golden halberd,
mounted his horse and suddenly recalled his
younger days,
set the horse's hoofs flying, scattering Qutang stones;
from White Emperor City, beyond river clouds,
hunched in the saddle, plunged eight thousand feet
straight down.
White-daubed walls pass like lightning, purple
reins slack,
east till I gain the level hills, emerge from soaring cliffs.
River hamlets, country houses, vie to be first in
my sight;
holding back the whip, easing the bit, I reach the
open highroad.
White-haired perhaps, but still able to astound
the populace,
remembering how well in my youth I could ride
and shoot—
how did I know that this fleet-footed mount, racing at
such speed,
red with sweat, straining, breathing out gobs of froth,

would unexpectedly stumble and land me in a
nasty spill?
In life, get too carried away and you meet much shame!
That's my chief sorrow as I lie on these quilts
and pillows,
plus the added ills and discomforts of old age.
Friends come to inquire. Brazen as I am,
with goosefoot cane I force myself to sit up, a servant
to lean on;
then, explanations over, we open our mouths and give
a big laugh.
They take my hand, sweep a special place by a bend of
the clear stream;
wine and meat heaped in mountains—off we go again!
As the feast begins, sad strings, huge flutes sounding,
together we point at the westering sun—won't be
with us much longer!
Amid much clamor, we drain our cups of filtered wine.
But why race your horses, coming to ask how I am?
As you well know,
Xi Kang, that nourisher of life, got himself executed—[1]

---

1. The poet Xi Kang (223–262) is famous for his philosophical essays, among them one on "Nourishing Life." Embroiled in a court quarrel, he was arrested, slandered, and condemned to execution. Du Fu ends his poem by merely pointing out this irony, but the implication clearly is: "Though I may be poor at 'nourishing life'—witness my fall from a horse—I don't go so far as to get myself killed."

Ninth Day

FIVE POEMS

(7-ch. regulated verse, first of five poems [only four in the set are extant]; probably written in the fall of 766 in Kuizhou, on the Double Ninth festival, held on the ninth day of the ninth month. On this day it was the custom for people to join with family and friends, climb to a high place, and drink wine with chrysanthemum blossoms floating in it to ensure good health. Du Fu, his health failing, observes the occasion alone. "Bamboo Leaf" in line 3 is a type of wine.)

119

Double Ninth, alone to pour the cup of wine;
lugging my ailments, I set off, climb the
 riverside terrace.
Bamboo Leaf, but not a sip of it for me;
from now on chrysanthemums no longer need bloom.
In this far-off quarter, sun setting, dark monkeys howl;
before the frost, from my homeland come wild
 geese, white.
No word from younger brothers and sister—where are
 they now?
Strife of arms, crippling age, both hurtle me onward!

Climbing to a High Place

(7-ch. regulated verse; on the same subject as the preceding poem, perhaps one of the "five poems" of that series.)

120

Wind shrill in the tall sky, gibbons wailing dolefully;
beaches clean, sands white, overhead the circling birds:
leaves fall, no end to them, rustling, rustling down;
ceaselessly the long river rushes, rushes on.
Autumn sorrow ten thousand miles from home, always
  a traveler;
sickness dogging each year of my life, I climb the
  terrace alone.
Troubles, vexations, coat my sidelocks with frost;
listless at this new blow, I forgo the cup of
  muddy wine.[1]

---

1. Because of illness, Du Fu was forced to give up the customary Double Ninth helping of wine.

Night in My Lodge

(7-ch. regulated verse; 766, in Kuizhou.)

121

Year ending, Yin and Yang hasten the already
brief daylight;
here at sky's edge, frost and snow, then clear
cold nights;
fifth watch drums and bugles, sad and militant sound;
over the Three Gorges, the Starry River, lights
moving, swaying.[1]
Weeping in the fields—a thousand households mourn
their battle-dead;
in how many places barbarian songs rise up from
fishermen and woodcutters?[2]
Sleeping Dragon, Prancing Horse, in the end,
yellow dust.[3]
Human affairs, word from others—I live utterly cut off
from these.

---

1. The fifth watch is around 4 A.M. The Starry River is the Milky Way; the swaying of its lights portends troubled times.
2. Songs sung by the non–Han Chinese inhabitants of the region.
3. Sleeping Dragon was the sobriquet of the Shu kingdom statesman Zhuge Liang (see poem 89); Prancing Horse was that of the Han period warlord and self-proclaimed emperor Gongsun Shu, the builder of White Emperor City.

Lone Wild Goose

(5-ch. regulated verse; late years.)

122

Lone wild goose, not drinking, not feeding,
flies crying, calls out his longing for the flock.
Who pities his lonely form,
lost from the others in ten-thousand-layered clouds?
I gaze to the end of gazing, still seem to see him;
so great my sorrow, I seem to hear him again,
while crows in the field, wholly unconcerned,
go on as before with their raucous cawing.

White-Little

(5-ch. regulated verse; late years. "White-little" is a small fish often eaten in the upper Yangzi region where Du Fu was living.)

123

White-little, one among the teeming species,
Heaven-destined two-inch fish,
tiny, frail, yet favored of water dwellers;
local custom treats you like a vegetable.
On sale in the fish stall, a jumble of silver blossoms;
dumped from a basket, snowflakes vanishing.
But those who value life leave the spawn untouched.
Taking spawn and all—what sense in that?

Autumn Fields

FIVE POEMS

(5-ch. regulated verse, the first, second, and third in the series; fall of 767, in Kuizhou.)

124

Autumn fields daily more overgrown,
cold river gliding under azure skies:
I've moored my boat to the Well Rope of the Man,[1]
settled in a house in a village of Chu.
Jujubes ripen—I leave others to pick them;
mallows grown straggly—I'd like to get at them with
  a hoe.[2]
Heaped on a plate, the old man's meal;
he sets aside a portion for fish in the stream.[3]

---

1. The "Well Rope" is a star that presides over the eastern Shu region where Du Fu was living, the old state of Chu. He uses the term "Man" (rhymes with the English word "wan") to allude to the non–Han Chinese inhabitants of the region.
2. Mallows were grown to be eaten.
3. Du Fu puts aside a portion as an offering to the fish, in accordance with the Buddhist teaching of the Flower Garland Sutra.

125

Easy to know—the law of this floating life;
hard to deflect a single being from it:
when waters are deep, fish are at their happiest,
where groves flourish, birds find their roost.
Old, feeble, I'm content to be poor and sickly,
wouldn't know how to deal with abundance.
Autumn winds blow over my armrest and cane;
I don't disdain fern sprouts from the
    northern mountain.[1]

---

1. A reference to the ancient sages Bo Yi and Shu Qi, who chose to live off the fern sprouts of Mt. Shouyang rather than compromise their principles.

126

Rites and music correct my shortcomings;[1]
mountains and forests offer enduring delight.
When I shake my head, my gauze cap tilts sideways;
when I sun my back, sunlight falls on my book.
I gather pine cones the wind has downed,
break open a honeycomb when skies are chill,
and coming on a few stray blossoms, red or blue,
halt my steps, bend close to their faint fragrance.

---

1. Rites and music are stressed in Confucianism as the inculcators of correct conduct and attitude.

Grieving Again
TWELVE POEMS

(5-ch. *jueju*, second in a series of twelve; 767, in Kuizhou.)

127

In ten thousand countries, still the horses of war;
my old homeland—what of it now?
That last journey back, friends so few;
already then, so many battlefields![1]

---

1. Du Fu is recalling the trip he made to the Luoyang region in 758, his last journey home.

Close of Day

(5-ch. regulated verse; 767, in Kuizhou.)

128

Cows and sheep hours ago down from the mountain,
each brushwood gate closed by now:
wind and moon in their own clear night,
but this river, these hills aren't my old home.
Rocky springs cascade over darkening cliffs,
dew on grasses soaks the autumn roots.
I, white-haired within the lamplight—
why does the wick make me all these flowers?[1]

---

1. The "flowers" are peculiar twistings of the wick that are said to foretell monetary gain. Du Fu doubts that such good fortune is on the way.

Another Poem for Wu Lang

(7-ch. regulated verse. In the fall of 767, Du Fu moved to a different location in Kuizhou and turned over his house in Rangxi to a kinsman named Wu Lang, who had apparently been assigned to a post in Kuizhou. Du Fu had been in the habit of leaving the jujubes that grew in front of his house for his neighbor to the west, an indigent old woman. In this poem to Wu Lang, to whom he had written an earlier poem, he asks Wu to continue this practice.)

129

Jujubes in front of my house—leave them for my
   western neighbor,
a lone housewife, no food, no sons.
If she weren't hard-pressed, she'd never dare
   touch them;
so fearful of giving offense, I pity her all the more.
You've come from far away, I don't like to interfere,
but running a fence between the two houses would
   be excessive.
She's told me how the officials have bled her to
   the bone—
thinking of what war does to us, my tears overflow.

Returning to East Camp After Staying for a Time at White Emperor

(5-ch. regulated verse; fall of 767, in Kuizhou, when Du Fu and his family, after a stay in Rangxi, here called White Emperor [City], returned to East Camp, where they had rice fields under cultivation.)

130

Back once more to our rice fields,
still the harvesting to be done.
We lay out a threshing ground, sorry for ant
  hills upturned;
leave the stray ears for village boys to glean.
Down comes the pestle, sunlight gleaming white;
off go the hulls from grains of rice red.
Eat hearty, best support for old age,
let a well-filled barn make up for our wanderings.

Visiting the Chan Master of Zhendi Temple

(5-ch. regulated verse; the site of Zhendi Temple, or the Temple of True Understanding, is uncertain, as is the date of the poem, though it undoubtedly dates from late in Du Fu's life.)

131

Monastery high in the mountains,
haze on its multilayered crags;
an icy spring threads among delicate rocks,
sunlit snow tumbles from tall pines.
Asking about the Dharma, I see the folly of poetry;
reflecting on the body, I lose my zest for wine.[1]
I could never cast aside wife and children,
but I might build a house near the first of your peaks.

---

1. Du Fu saw his attachment to wine and poetry as two "offenses" that he would have to remedy if he were to become a sincere Buddhist follower. Whether he ever seriously considered giving them up is questionable.

Climbing Yueyang Tower

(5-ch. regulated verse; in late winter, 768, when Du Fu climbed the three-story tower overlooking Lake Dongting at the west gate of Yueyang in Hunan. Wu and Chu are ancient names for the regions of eastern and southern China, respectively.)

132

Long ago I heard of Lake Dongting,
now I climb Yueyang Tower:
Wu and Chu slope off to south and east,
Heaven and Earth day and night float on these waters.
Of kinfolk, friends, not one word,
old, sickly, in my solitary boat,
and north of the barrier mountains the fighting
   goes on—
as I lean on the railing, tears stream down.

Yangzi and Han

(5-ch. regulated verse; probably written in the fall of 769, when the poet reached the region around the confluence of the Yangzi and Han rivers in Hubei.)

133

Yangzi and Han, thoughts of a homebound traveler;
Heaven and Earth and one stale pedant:
scattered clouds in a sky far away as I am;
long night, the moon alone like me.
In setting sun, my mind agile as ever;
autumn wind, yet my ailments are on the mend.
Hold on to an old horse—they did that in past times,
though he's no more good for the long haul.[1]

---

1. Reference to a story in *Han Feizi*, sec. 22, about how an official, having become lost in the mountains, used an old horse to help him find the way home.

On Meeting Li Guinian in the Region South of the Yangzi

(7-ch. *jueju*; 770, at Tanzhou in Hunan. Li Guinian was a famous singer who had enjoyed favor under Emperor Xuanzong. Prince Qi was a younger brother of Emperor Xuanzong and a noted patron of the arts.)

134
I always used to see you at Prince Qi's mansion,
heard you how many times at Lord Cui's home?
Now when the scenery is finest here south of
    the Yangzi,
that we should meet once more just as blossoms
    are falling!

Little Cold Food, Written Aboard the Boat

(7-ch. regulated verse; 770. Little Cold Food was the day after the Cold Food Festival, held on the 105th day after the winter solstice, when cooking fires were extinguished and only cold food was eaten for three days. The pheasant cap in line 2 was worn by elderly men.)

135

Festive morning: I make myself drink a little, food
still cold,
lean on the armrest, downcast, wearing a
pheasant cap:
boat on the spring waters, like sitting on top of the sky;
blossoms of my old age, seen as though through mist.[1]
A playful butterfly, graceful, threads through the
silent curtains;
nimble gulls one by one swoop over rapid shallows.
Clouds white, mountains green, ten thousand
miles away,
I gaze straight north, grieving—Chang'an there!

---

1. Because of his failing eyesight he can barely make out the springtime blossoms.

selected Bibliography

Allen, Rewi. *Tu Fu: Selected Poems*. Beijing: Foreign Languages Press, 1962.

Ayscough, Florence. *Tu Fu: The Autobiography of a Chinese Poet,*. Vol. I, A.D. 712–759. Boston: Houghton Mifflin, 1929.

——. *Travels of a Chinese Poet: Tu Fu, Guest of Rivers and Lakes*. Vol. II, A.D. 759–770. Boston: Houghton Mifflin, 1934.

Chou, Eva Shan. *Reconsidering Tu Fu: Literary Greatness and Cultural Context*. Cambridge: Cambridge University Press, 1995.

Cooper, Arthur. *Li Po and Tu Fu*. Baltimore: Penguin, 1965.

Davis, A. R. *Tu Fu*. New York: Twayne, 1971.

Graham, A. C. *Poems of the Late T'ang*. Baltimore: Penguin, 1965.

Hawkes, David. *A Little Primer of Tu Fu*. Oxford: Oxford University Press, 1967; Hong Kong: Chinese University of Hong Kong, Renditions Paperback, 1987.

Hinton, David. *The Selected Poems of Tu Fu*. New York: New Directions, 1989.

Hung, William. *Tu Fu: China's Greatest Poet*. Cambridge: Harvard University Press, 1952.

Lattimore, David. *Harmony of the World*. Providence: Copper Beech Press, 1980.

McCraw, David R. *Du Fu's Laments from the South*. Honolulu: University of Hawaii Press, 1992.

Mei, Tsu-lin and Yu-kung Kao, "Tu Fu's 'Autumn Meditations': An Exercise in Linguistic Criticism." *Harvard Journal of Asiatic Studies* 28 (1968): 44–80.

Owen, Stephen. *The Great Age of Chinese Poetry: The High T'ang*. New Haven: Yale University Press, 1981.

Rexroth, Kenneth. *One Hundred Poems from the Chinese*. New York: New Directions, 1971.

Seaton, J. P. and James Cryer. *Bright Moon, Perching Bird: Poems by Li Po and Tu Fu*. Middletown, Conn.: Wesleyan University Press, 1987.

Translations from the Asian Classics

Major Plays of Chikamatsu, tr. Donald Keene 1961

Four Major Plays of Chikamatsu, tr. Donald Keene. Paperback ed. only. 1961; rev. ed. 1997

Records of the Grand Historian of China, translated from the Shih chi of Ssu-ma Ch'ien, tr. Burton Watson, 2 vols. 1961

Instructions for Practical Living and Other Neo-Confucian Writings by Wang Yang-ming, tr. Wing-tsit Chan 1963

Hsün Tzu: Basic Writings, tr. Burton Watson, paperback ed. only. 1963; rev. ed. 1996

Chuang Tzu: Basic Writings, tr. Burton Watson, paperback ed. only. 1964; rev. ed. 1996

The Mahābhārata, tr. Chakravarthi V. Narasimhan. Also in paperback ed. 1965; rev. ed. 1997

The Manyōshū, Nippon Gakujutsu Shinkōkai edition 1965

Su Tung-p'o: Selections from a Sung Dynasty Poet, tr. Burton Watson. Also in paperback ed. 1965

Bhartrihari: Poems, tr. Barbara Stoler Miller. Also in paperback ed. 1967

Basic Writings of Mo Tzu, Hsün Tzu, and Han Fei Tzu, tr. Burton Watson. Also in separate paperback eds. 1967

The Awakening of Faith, Attributed to Aśvaghosha, tr. Yoshito S. Hakeda. Also in paperback ed. 1967

Reflections on Things at Hand: The Neo-Confucian Anthology, comp. Chu Hsi and Lü Tsu-ch'ien, tr. Wing-tsit Chan 1967

The Platform Sutra of the Sixth Patriarch, tr. Philip B. Yampolsky. Also in paperback ed. 1967

Essays in Idleness: The Tsurezuregusa of Kenkō, tr. Donald Keene. Also in paperback ed. 1967

The Pillow Book of Sei Shōnagon, tr. Ivan Morris, 2 vols. 1967

Two Plays of Ancient India: The Little Clay Cart and the Minister's Seal, tr. J. A. B. van Buitenen 1968

The Complete Works of Chuang Tzu, tr. Burton Watson 1968

The Romance of the Western Chamber (Hsi Hsiang chi), tr. S. I. Hsiung. Also in paperback ed. 1968

The Manyōshū, Nippon Gakujutsu Shinkōkai edition. Paperback ed. only. 1969

Records of the Historian: Chapters from the Shih chi of Ssu-ma Ch'ien, tr. Burton Watson. Paperback ed. only. 1969

Cold Mountain: 100 Poems by the T'ang Poet Han-shan, tr. Burton Watson. Also in paperback ed. 1970

Twenty Plays of the Nō Theatre, ed. Donald Keene. Also in paperback ed. 1970

Chūshingura: The Treasury of Loyal Retainers, tr. Donald Keene. Also in paperback ed. 1971; rev. ed. 1997

The Zen Master Hakuin: Selected Writings, tr. Philip B. Yampolsky 1971

Chinese Rhyme-Prose: Poems in the Fu Form from the Han and Six Dynasties Periods, tr. Burton Watson. Also in paperback ed. 1971

Kūkai: Major Works, tr. Yoshito S. Hakeda. Also in paperback ed. 1972

The Old Man Who Does as He Pleases: Selections from the Poetry and Prose of Lu Yu, tr. Burton Watson 1973

The Lion's Roar of Queen Śrīmālā, tr. Alex and Hideko Wayman 1974

Courtier and Commoner in Ancient China: Selections from the History of the Former Han by Pan Ku, tr. Burton Watson. Also in paperback ed. 1974

Japanese Literature in Chinese, vol. 1: *Poetry and Prose in Chinese by Japanese Writers of the Early Period*, tr. Burton Watson 1975

Japanese Literature in Chinese, vol. 2: *Poetry and Prose in Chinese by Japanese Writers of the Later Period*, tr. Burton Watson 1976

Scripture of the Lotus Blossom of the Fine Dharma, tr. Leon Hurvitz. Also in paperback ed. 1976

Love Song of the Dark Lord: Jayadeva's Gītagovinda, tr. Barbara Stoler Miller. Also in paperback ed. Cloth ed. includes critical text of the Sanskrit. 1977; rev. ed. 1997

Ryōkan: Zen Monk-Poet of Japan, tr. Burton Watson 1977

Calming the Mind and Discerning the Real: From the Lam rim chen mo of Tsoṇ-kha-pa, tr. Alex Wayman 1978

The Hermit and the Love-Thief: Sanskrit Poems of Bhartrihari and Bilhaṇa, tr. Barbara Stoler Miller 1978

The Lute: Kao Ming's P'i-p'a chi, tr. Jean Mulligan. Also in paperback ed. 1980

A Chronicle of Gods and Sovereigns: Jinnō Shōtōki of Kitabatake Chikafusa, tr. H. Paul Varley 1980

Among the Flowers: The Hua-chien chi, tr. Lois Fusek 1982

Grass Hill: Poems and Prose by the Japanese Monk Gensei, tr. Burton Watson 1983

Doctors, Diviners, and Magicians of Ancient China: Biographies of Fang-shih, tr. Kenneth J. DeWoskin. Also in paperback ed. 1983

Theater of Memory: The Plays of Kālidāsa, ed. Barbara Stoler Miller. Also in paperback ed. 1984

The Columbia Book of Chinese Poetry: From Early Times to the Thirteenth Century, ed. and tr. Burton Watson. Also in paperback ed. 1984

Poems of Love and War: From the Eight Anthologies and the Ten Long Poems of Classical Tamil, tr. A. K. Ramanujan. Also in paperback ed. 1985

The Bhagavad Gita: Krishna's Counsel in Time of War, tr. Barbara Stoler Miller 1986

The Columbia Book of Later Chinese Poetry, ed. and tr. Jonathan Chaves. Also in paperback ed. 1986

The Tso Chuan: Selections from China's Oldest Narrative History, tr. Burton Watson 1989

Waiting for the Wind: Thirty-six Poets of Japan's Late Medieval Age, tr. Steven Carter 1989

Selected Writings of Nichiren, ed. Philip B. Yampolsky 1990

Saigyō, Poems of a Mountain Home, tr. Burton Watson 1990

The Book of Lieh Tzu: A Classic of the Tao, tr. A. C. Graham. Morningside ed. 1990

The Tale of an Anklet: An Epic of South India—The Cilappatikāram of Iḷaṇkō Aṭikaḷ, tr. R. Parthasarathy 1993

Waiting for the Dawn: A Plan for the Prince, tr. and introduction by Wm. Theodore de Bary 1993

Yoshitsune and the Thousand Cherry Trees: A Masterpiece of the Eighteenth-Century Japanese Puppet Theater, tr., annotated, and with introduction by Stanleigh H. Jones, Jr. 1993

The Lotus Sutra, tr. Burton Watson. Also in paperback ed. 1993

The Classic of Changes: A New Translation of the I Ching as Interpreted by Wang Bi, tr. Richard John Lynn 1994

Beyond Spring: Tz'u Poems of the Sung Dynasty, tr. Julie Landau 1994

The Columbia Anthology of Traditional Chinese Literature, ed. Victor H. Mair 1994

Scenes for Mandarins: The Elite Theater of the Ming, tr. Cyril Birch 1995

Letters of Nichiren, ed. Philip B. Yampolsky; tr. Burton Watson et al. 1996

Unforgotten Dreams: Poems by the Zen Monk Shōtetsu, tr. Steven D. Carter 1997

The Vimalakirti Sutra, tr. Burton Watson 1997

Japanese and Chinese Poems to Sing: The Wakan rōei shū, tr. J. Thomas Rimer and Jonathan Chaves 1997

A Tower for the Summer Heat, Li Yu, tr. Patrick Hanan 1998

Traditional Japanese Theater: An Anthology of Plays, Karen Brazell 1998

The Original Analects: Sayings of Confucius and His Successors (0479–0249), E. Bruce Brooks and A. Taeko Brooks 1998

The Classic of the Way and Virtue: A New Translation of the Tao-te ching *of Laozi as Interpreted by Wang Bi*, tr. Richard John Lynn 1999

The Four Hundred Songs of War and Wisdom: An Anthology of Poems from Classical Tamil, The Puranāṇūṛu, eds. and trans. George L. Hart and Hank Heifetz 1999

Original Tao: Inward Training (Nei-yeh) *and the Foundations of Taoist Mysticism*, by Harold D. Roth 1999

Lao Tzu's Tao Te Ching*: A Translation of the Startling New Documents Found at Guodian*, Robert G. Henricks 2000

The Shorter Columbia Anthology of Traditional Chinese Literature, ed. Victor H. Mair 2000

Mistress and Maid (Jiaohongji) by Meng Chengshun, tr. Cyril Birch 2001

Chikamatsu: Five Late Plays, tr. and ed. C. Andrew Gerstle

The Essential Lotus: Selections from the Lotus Sutra, tr. Burton Watson 2002

Early Modern Japanese Literature: An Anthology, 1600–1900, ed. Haruo Shirane 2002

MODERN ASIAN LITERATURE

Modern Japanese Drama: An Anthology, ed. and tr. Ted. Takaya. Also in paperback ed. 1979

Mask and Sword: Two Plays for the Contemporary Japanese Theater, by Yamazaki Masakazu, tr. J. Thomas Rimer 1980

Yokomitsu Riichi, Modernist, Dennis Keene 1980

Nepali Visions, Nepali Dreams: The Poetry of Laxmiprasad Devkota, tr. David Rubin 1980

Literature of the Hundred Flowers, vol. 1: *Criticism and Polemics*, ed. Hualing Nieh 1981

Literature of the Hundred Flowers, vol. 2: *Poetry and Fiction*, ed. Hualing Nieh 1981

Modern Chinese Stories and Novellas, 1919 1949, ed. Joseph S. M. Lau, C. T. Hsia, and Leo Ou-fan Lee. Also in paperback ed. 1984

A View by the Sea, by Yasuoka Shōtarō, tr. Kären Wigen Lewis 1984

Other Worlds: Arishima Takeo and the Bounds of Modern Japanese Fiction, by Paul Anderer 1984

Selected Poems of Sō Chōngju, tr. with introduction by David R. McCann 1989

The Sting of Life: Four Contemporary Japanese Novelists, by Van C. Gessel 1989

Stories of Osaka Life, by Oda Sakunosuke, tr. Burton Watson 1990

The Bodhisattva, or Samantabhadra, by Ishikawa Jun, tr. with introduction by William Jefferson Tyler 1990

The Travels of Lao Ts'an, by Liu T'ieh-yün, tr. Harold Shadick. Morningside ed. 1990

Three Plays by Kōbō Abe, tr. with introduction by Donald Keene 1993

The Columbia Anthology of Modern Chinese Literature, ed. Joseph S. M. Lau and Howard Goldblatt 1995

Modern Japanese Tanka, ed. and tr. by Makoto Ueda 1996

Masaoka Shiki: Selected Poems, ed. and tr. by Burton Watson 1997

Writing Women in Modern China: An Anthology of Women's Literature from the Early Twentieth Century, ed. and tr. by Amy D. Dooling and Kristina M. Torgeson 1998

American Stories, by Nagai Kafū, tr. Mitsuko Iriye 2000

The Paper Door and Other Stories, by Shiga Naoya, tr. Lane Dunlop 2001

Grass for My Pillow, by Saiichi Maruya, tr. Dennis Keene 2002

STUDIES IN ASIAN CULTURE

The Ōnin War: History of Its Origins and Background, with a Selective Translation of the Chronicle of Ōnin, by H. Paul Varley 1967

Chinese Government in Ming Times: Seven Studies, ed. Charles O. Hucker 1969

The Actors' Analects (Yakusha Rongo), ed. and tr. by Charles J. Dunn and Bungō Torigoe 1969

Self and Society in Ming Thought, by Wm. Theodore de Bary and the Conference on Ming Thought. Also in paperback ed. 1970

A History of Islamic Philosophy, by Majid Fakhry, 2d ed. 1983

Phantasies of a Love Thief: The Caurapañatcāśikā Attributed to Bilhaṇa, by Barbara Stoler Miller 1971

Iqbal: Poet-Philosopher of Pakistan, ed. Hafeez Malik 1971

The Golden Tradition: An Anthology of Urdu Poetry, ed. and tr. Ahmed Ali. Also in paperback ed. 1973

Conquerors and Confucians: Aspects of Political Change in Late Yüan China, by John W. Dardess 1973

The Unfolding of Neo-Confucianism, by Wm. Theodore de Bary and the Conference on Seventeenth-Century Chinese Thought. Also in paperback ed. 1975

To Acquire Wisdom: The Way of Wang Yang-ming, by Julia Ching 1976

Gods, Priests, and Warriors: The Bhṛgus of the Mahābhārata, by Robert P. Goldman 1977

Mei Yao-ch'en and the Development of Early Sung Poetry, by Jonathan Chaves 1976

The Legend of Semimaru, Blind Musician of Japan, by Susan Matisoff 1977

Sir Sayyid Ahmad Khan and Muslim Modernization in India and Pakistan, by Hafeez Malik 1980

The Khilafat Movement: Religious Symbolism and Political Mobilization in India, by Gail Minault 1982

The World of K'ung Shang-jen: A Man of Letters in Early Ch'ing China, by Richard Strassberg 1983

The Lotus Boat: The Origins of Chinese Tz'u Poetry in T'ang Popular Culture, by Marsha L. Wagner 1984

Expressions of Self in Chinese Literature, ed. Robert E. Hegel and Richard C. Hessney 1985

Songs for the Bride: Women's Voices and Wedding Rites of Rural India, by W. G. Archer; eds. Barbara Stoler Miller and Mildred Archer 1986

The Confucian Kingship in Korea: Yongjo and the Politics of Sagacity, by JaHyun Kim Haboush 1988

COMPANIONS TO ASIAN STUDIES

Approaches to the Oriental Classics, ed. Wm. Theodore de Bary 1959

Early Chinese Literature, by Burton Watson. Also in paperback ed. 1962

Approaches to Asian Civilizations, eds. Wm. Theodore de Bary and Ainslie T. Embree 1964

The Classic Chinese Novel: A Critical Introduction, by C. T. Hsia. Also in paperback ed. 1968

Chinese Lyricism: Shih Poetry from the Second to the Twelfth Century, tr. Burton Watson. Also in paperback ed. 1971

A Syllabus of Indian Civilization, by Leonard A. Gordon and Barbara Stoler Miller 1971

Twentieth-Century Chinese Stories, ed. C. T. Hsia and Joseph S. M. Lau. Also in paperback ed. 1971

A Syllabus of Chinese Civilization, by J. Mason Gentzler, 2d ed. 1972

A Syllabus of Japanese Civilization, by H. Paul Varley, 2d ed. 1972

An Introduction to Chinese Civilization, ed. John Meskill, with the assistance of J. Mason Gentzler 1973

An Introduction to Japanese Civilization, ed. Arthur E. Tiedemann 1974

Ukifune: Love in the Tale of Genji, ed. Andrew Pekarik 1982

The Pleasures of Japanese Literature, by Donald Keene 1988

A Guide to Oriental Classics, eds. Wm. Theodore de Bary and Ainslie T. Embree; 3d edition ed. Amy Vladeck Heinrich, 2 vols. 1989

INTRODUCTION TO ASIAN CIVILIZATIONS

WM. THEODORE DE BARY, GENERAL EDITOR

Sources of Japanese Tradition, 1958; paperback ed., 2 vols., 1964. 2d ed., vol. 1, 2001, compiled by Wm. Theodore de Bary, Donald Keene, George Tanabe, and Paul Varley

Sources of Indian Tradition, 1958; paperback ed., 2 vols., 1964. 2d ed., 2 vols., 1988

Sources of Chinese Tradition, 1960, paperback ed., 2 vols., 1964. 2d ed., vol. 1, 1999, compiled by Wm. Theodore de Bary and Irene Bloom; vol. 2, 2000, compiled by Wm. Theodore de Bary and Richard Lufrano

Sources of Korean Tradition, 1997; 2 vols., vol. 1, 1997, compiled by Peter H. Lee and Wm. Theodore de Bary; vol. 2, 2001, compiled by Yongho Ch'oe, Peter H. Lee, and Wm. Theodore de Bary

NEO-CONFUCIAN STUDIES

Instructions for Practical Living and Other Neo-Confucian Writings by Wang Yang-ming, tr. Wing-tsit Chan 1963

Reflections on Things at Hand: The Neo-Confucian Anthology, comp. Chu Hsi and Lü Tsu-ch'ien, tr. Wing-tsit Chan 1967

Self and Society in Ming Thought, by Wm. Theodore de Bary and the Conference on Ming Thought. Also in paperback ed. 1970

The Unfolding of Neo-Confucianism, by Wm. Theodore de Bary and the Conference on Seventeenth-Century Chinese Thought. Also in paperback ed. 1975

Principle and Practicality: Essays in Neo-Confucianism and Practical Learning, eds. Wm. Theodore de Bary and Irene Bloom. Also in paperback ed. 1979

The Syncretic Religion of Lin Chao-en, by Judith A. Berling 1980

The Renewal of Buddhism in China: Chu-hung and the Late Ming Synthesis, by Chün-fang Yü 1981

Neo-Confucian Orthodoxy and the Learning of the Mind-and-Heart, by Wm. Theodore de Bary 1981

Yüan Thought: Chinese Thought and Religion Under the Mongols, eds. Hok-lam Chan and Wm. Theodore de Bary 1982

The Liberal Tradition in China, by Wm. Theodore de Bary 1983

The Development and Decline of Chinese Cosmology, by John B. Henderson 1984

The Rise of Neo-Confucianism in Korea, by Wm. Theodore de Bary and JaHyun Kim Haboush 1985

Chiao Hung and the Restructuring of Neo-Confucianism in Late Ming, by Edward T. Ch'ien 1985

Neo-Confucian Terms Explained: Pei-hsi tzu-i, by Ch'en Ch'un, ed. and trans. Wing-tsit Chan 1986

Knowledge Painfully Acquired: K'un-chih chi, by Lo Ch'in-shun, ed. and trans. Irene Bloom 1987

To Become a Sage: The Ten Diagrams on Sage Learning, by Yi T'oegye, ed. and trans. Michael C. Kalton 1988

The Message of the Mind in Neo-Confucian Thought, by Wm. Theodore de Bary 1989

Lightning Source UK Ltd.
Milton Keynes UK
UKHW012141180321
380593UK00002B/169